Conversations with Atlantis 2000 - 2010 (and beyond)

Published by Moon Publishing, Nollaig McKeogh
Carrowkeel View
Laragan
Callooney
Co-Sligo
Ireland
Channel4atlantis@googlemail.com

Copyright

All rights reserved.

No part of this work may be reproduced without the prior permission of the author.

© Nollaig A T McKeogh 2009

Cover design by Publishack.com
Printed and bound by Publishack.com - Valencia, Spain.

Note

The writings contained in this publication are delivered with the intention to be both educational and therapeutic. They are not for diagnosis or self-treatment of any health disorder under any circumstances. The information is channelled through in good faith and no liability will be accepted for any loss or expense incurred through the misuse of the material.

Conversations with Atlantis
2000 - 2010 (and beyond)

NOLLAIG McKEOGH

Contents

Introduction & Profile   13

Year 2000 - New Millennium   19

A New Millennium…Equality, Enlightenment, Climate Change and Truth

Salamander Pure Essence

Reiki Energy

Year 2001   28

Foot and Mouth Disease

E.E.C. - The Art of Listening and People

Refugees and Asylum Seekers

Negative and Positive Thought Process

The New Golden Age – Shock treatment, Corruption, Governments and Power

Purity

Own Divinity

Christ Consciousness

Lessons State of Mankind

Confirmations of My Mission

Atlantis in relation to Spiritual Aspects of Man

Thought Process and Vibration – Help with our Salvation

Important Message for You

Cordoba, Spain and Love Poem

Year 2002

A Time to Explore

London Thames Barrier

Communication of the spirit compared with physical communication

Tolerance

Communication on a Spiritual Plane

School of Light

Europe – Corruption and Drugs

Trust and Lessons with Free Will

Rise above Conflict

Meditation

Schools of Light, Forgiveness

Travel Good Cheap for a Time Only

Euro and Corruption in banks

Drugs

Conflict

Repentance and Forgiveness

Verona a target

Teaching of the Ascended Masters, Order of Melchizedek and Verona

Year 2003

A Time to Let Go and Just Be

Ascension Process

Atlantis a Lost Civilisation

Justice

Iraq and Saddam

Inspiration and Knowledge

Meditation

Atlantian Civilisation Advice

Torture

Peace to soul

Transformation Programme and Circles of Light

Music

Dominance

Atlantian Lifestyle

Democracy

World Leaders and Greed

Challenge

Ireland Costly to live

Life on Earth

Year 2004

Atlantians made mistakes

Infinity

Poem titled Religion

The Crystalline Energy Field

Politics

Nuclear weapons a threat to the west

Trouble to England

People

Atlantians' Use of Solar and Wind Energy

Climate

Year 2005

Great to be Alive East-West Relations 2005-2009 Warning

Warning in Relation to Terror

Letter to Downing Street November 2005

Pope John Paul

Inflation 2005-2009

Turkey in East/West Relations

The figure 8 and the Eight Meditation

Healing for Atlantis

Fortunes

Errors in Humanity and Karma

Poetry

Oil

Atlantis Essence

Matrix of the Body

Matrix of the Planet

Purity of Atlantis

People and the way of the world

Humanity in relation to governments 2006-2009 and beyond

Climate

Knowledge

Human Trafficking

Year 2006

Mankind is in need of a long term fix

The changing face of our planet

Ascended masters and the violet flame

Hamas

Global warming 2006-2016

Peace, love and light

Evolution

Property and rising house rates

Honesty

Divinity

Year 2007 111

Atlantis Connects Direct from Heaven

Tough Time Ahead

Attitudes

Coming Events in Spain

Purity in the Atlantian Essence

St. Germain

The Holy Spirit

Christian faith in Ireland being lost within Europe

Year 2008 117

Fear is the absence of love

Evolution in Africa

Coming events in Ireland 2008-2010

China and Control

Burma in a state of fear and control and Poem 'Angel of Burma'

Year 2009 *123*

This millennium is a change in consciousness

Church needs to humble itself at the core

A wonderful time for growth, through saintly help 2009 to 2012

American President Barrack H Obama

Year 2010 *128*

Please commit to our mission

Nuclear gases must be blocked

Testimonials *131*
Poetry & Mediatation *143*
Planet Earth *160*
Mini Glossary *163*

Atlantis

An inspirational journey
and direct communication with a lost, highly evolved civilisation: the Atlantians.

They warn mankind of their mistakes while living on earth and wish to help with our evolution and the planet's part in this. The time is correct now!
To transform, re-connect to our Divinity and allow the Golden Age to reign once again:
Each soul has a part to play in this great process.

Listen and you will hear.

It is the correct evolutionary time,
to let go of all your fear.

Take back your personal power now –
by becoming in Self Truth

By
Nollaig McKeogh

The Wisdom Teachings of the Atlantians

Words of truth by Saint Germain the Ascended Master Jacob and all his helpers in the spirit world.

"I am a simple channel,
no more, no less"

Introduction and Profile

Nollaig McKeogh was born in Limerick city, a native of Ballina, Co. Tipperary, she now lives in Co. Sligo, Ireland - a writer's haven which inspired the world-famous W.B. Yeats to write award-winning poetry. The county is known for its sacred burial grounds, rugged coastline, mystic terrain, Benbulben and sacred Irishmurray Island off the Sligo coast, near magical Mullaghmore.

Nollaig is a colour, crystal and meditation therapist and has received diplomas from the British School of Yoga. She is also a therapeutic touch healer and holistic workshop coordinator, having trained at the University College, Galway.

Nollaig is a member of the association of freelance writers, having studied with the Writers' Bureau, Manchester. She is the author and co-author of meditations printed in the meditation section of this book.

Nollaig is currently involved with the setting up of holistic circles.

- **Circle of Light and Planetary Healing for those who feel ready and committed to this mission**
- **Inspirational Writers Circle**
- **Healing and Colour**
- **Holistic Support Therapy Exchange Network Circle**
- **Atlantis Workshops and Holistic Coaching, which includes spiritual guidance on all walks of life**
- **Heritage Charity Walkers Circle, The Peacock Ramblers Network Club**

   Email: channel4atlantis@googlemail.com

Acknowledgements

This book is dedicated to the Atlantians, our forbearers who once lived in harmony with each other, with the planet and connected to Divinity. To St. Germain, ascended Master responsible for the transformation plan on earth at this time. Jacob and many helpers in the light world for their guidance and patience in delivering the sacred writings.

To the ascended ones I owe much gratitude. To my father Pat in spirit who through direct communication in light, abolished all fear and allowed me to share the ultimate joy that awaits all enlightened souls, on their journey onwards.

To the staff of the Youth Information Centre, Sligo. Thank you for your patience, time and hard work.

To my publishing colleagues. Your expertise has made writing it a therapeutic art. To those associated with helping to ground this material and bring this book into form.

Last but not least my husband John V who supported, listened and encouraged me to keep on my path. My dear mother Peig and sisters who often do not want to listen but always acknowledged the true gift from above.

To my treasured and holistic friends who supported the circles and the Atlantian plight over the years. Thanks for the prayers and trust in my spirited openness.

To Sligo Credit Union, a friend to the environment. Thank you to Barry for your help with sponsorship.

To all who acknowledged my work as a channel it is both encouraging and very rewarding to those who listen.

My Conversations with Atlantis first began as we approached the new millennium. Having set up a holistic practice at Knock (Co. Mayo, Ireland) with a view to bringing like-minded people together to work with the vision of healing mind, body and soul using the vibrations of colour, crystals, energy, massage, meditation, counselling, nutrition and whatever possible to bring about much needed balance to clients. Educational holistic workshops were also included in my great plan with a vision to set up a holistic support therapy exchange group in order for healers to share and recharge their overworked batteries.

It was a project close to my heart and at that time I was ready for the challenge.

On my return home to mystical Sligo after an enlightening day of therapy treatments. I felt inspired to write. Putting pen to paper I began to draw circles ooooooooooo. This is the way our circle goes, this is very important.

At this stage conversations began between the highly evolved civilisation and myself.

The question-answer conversational format is as follows:
N: Nollaig
A: Atlantis

Nollaig (N): Why is this so important please?

Atlantis (A): Because energy is generated this way on earth and no other.

N: Who are you please?

A: We are your energy directors, if you like, from the Atlantian source.

N: Tell me something about your source please?

A: Our source was the highest, brightest, oldest and most crystal type ever to exist on earth. Clear in our purpose for the renewal and regeneration of the New World. Bringing old knowledge that you already have, but lost through negative thinking. Is that clear?

N: Yes, what should I do next?

A: Just wait and you will know when you meet with others, as all have similar knowledge but it needs to be in numbers to generate the power needed in order to shift consciousness, to a new way of thinking, acting, working being, etc. A newness, freshness, lightness in people is needed for enlightenment and change.

N: Is that all?

A: For now yes

N: I give thanks

A New Millennium Approaches
Mankind Needs Life Coaching

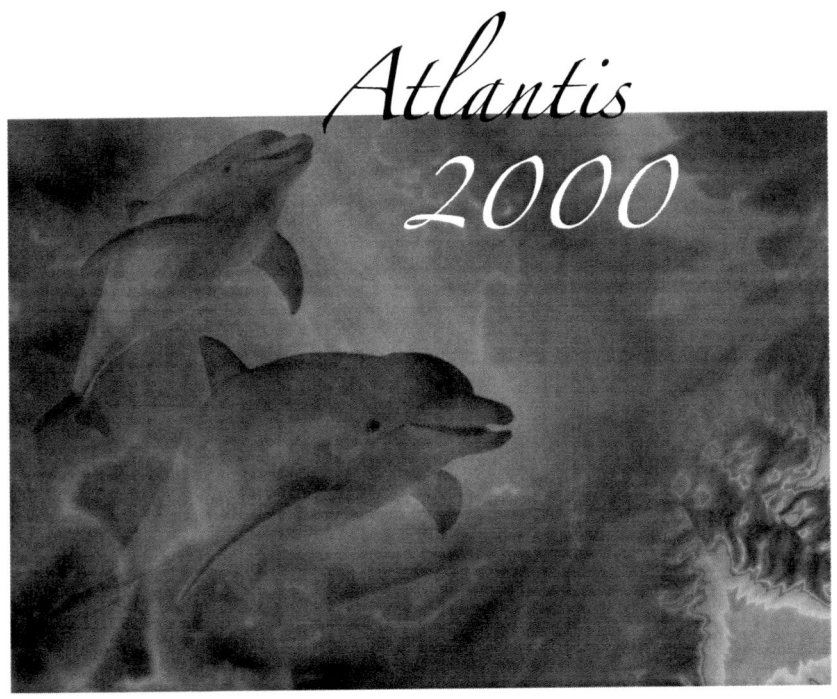

Year 2000 - Equality

Today we would like to discuss Equality.
It is important to know that equality is favoured in the golden age. All people are equal on earth. Do not look up to or down on anybody, this is all part of the old age now, the material world is crumbling at the moment. It is happening in all governments in the world, no truth in matters. All false and greed. England, America, Russia, Ireland and all over Europe. It must change now and the people are the ones to change this by not voting and accepting the old anymore. Being in own truth and knowing what is correct is all important now. Is that clear my child?

N: Yes, very clear, I give thanks.

A: Today we wish to talk on the planet.

N: Go ahead please.

A: Climate change affects humanity as humanity affects climate change. The time is correct now to stop. To give back to the planet and to think in a different way. The choice is ours to destroy or to build. All will be revealed soon: Build now and renew.

N: Why did The Hague meeting breakdown?

A: Because man is so proud and stuck in the self and in woman, he does not put planet first, time is near to cleanse soon: A number of years to put the planet in order, be in own power and light now, part of all that is.

N: I give thanks.

Enlightenment

A: We would now like to talk on Enlightenment.

N: Go ahead please.

A: Check out the Cathar prophecy. Is it about enlightenment to all at being at one with the planet, love is the core of all. Once again do not look up to or down upon other souls, this is very important. Dictatorship is finished. It never was the way forward - hierarchy, fear, undercover, closed attitudes and snobbery etc. This is over, it is last century stuff. Unity now as all people are equal on the planet. Love draws out the healing power in all. Love and acceptance of self is the root of all power and healing, mankind needs to understand this. Each person will carry the light. Recognise God in self number one, and in others number two. Is that clear my child?

N: Yes.

A: We will continue. The old church is about dictating from a high in a physical plant, which is ego related, hence fear and closure. Openness is the key to growth. This era is about openness. Th e human being has potential beyond that of worship. Is that understood my child?

N: No, clarification please.

A: Recognise divinity within: One cannot recognise it in priests, bishops, nuns, popes or others until recognised in the self. All are human and all are weak, and all are on paths. We cannot condemn, criticise, or judge anybody, any religion or anything until we are true to our self. Some are not yet in self truth and aspiring to the same. Understand?

N: Yes, I give thanks.

Truth

A: Today we wish to discuss Truth.

Affirmation for you to share.

(I seek the truth in understanding my experiences).

N: Go ahead please.

Affirmation

Power is in truth and in the moment

We cannot standby and take others' truth, this is very important.

Truth is in the self - we refer to this as self truth.

Use this, it is called taking back our power.

Truth is paramount now

Work on thinking thought process

It is time for change

Transformation is now, it is happening

Those who are not ready in truth… are held back

N: What do you mean by 'held back' please?

A: Well caught up in either the material world, materialism or with partners' partner and materialism is the source of negativity. It is rampant and it is in the now but changing. Fear, TV, etc. Celebrate humanity, celebrate your senses. What is my truth? Is humanity going to stand by and watch truth die so easily?

I am the truth (always use in love and light). A good affirmation, you will know that one day truth is all there is. No truth, no person: The soul seeks truth always. Truth is paramount in the evaluation of man:

Truth is the ultimate. Man must become truth and truth will win: No falsehood, here or any place. It is over it is not working, not the way forward now. Truth is all.

N: I give thanks.

A: Good morning. It is important to know that all will be revealed to you when the time is correct.

N: What do you mean?

A: All information for the planet e.g. oil, hurricanes, things that have to happen re-cleansing negativity in order for the Golden Age to come about.

N: When please?

A: Do not know exact time yet, do not panic my child, be for now. You are protected and guided all the time.

N: Anything else?

A: No,

N: I give thanks.

N: Good morning, do you have a message please?

A: Now at this time we would like to discuss self growth. You will benefit much by focusing. By being, and stop thinking about others. As all are on paths, healers are now turning to correct paths. You are commissioned to help with this earthly duty. It is good work. It is urgent work and it must happen soon:

N: Explain please?

A: The world is in much trouble. To know that all will take action in the near future.

N: What do you mean?

A: All environmental issues.

N: What do you mean by 'action'? Please clarify.

A: Action: By that we mean clearing of negativity.

N: How will that happen?

A: By means of storms and snow storms, ice.

N: Where please?

A: Northern Europe, Scotland, N: Ireland, Yorkshire and Jersey floods.

N: Any place else?

A: Yes, London:

N: What will happen in the near future? I need clarification:

A: Well things will happen quickly by way of hurricanes, floods and ice breaking causing the floods the seas to rise and currents

N: Where please?

A: Irish Atlantic.

N: When will this happen?

A: : Soon:

N: Advice please.

A: Nothing is necessary, this must happen to quieten mankind. Please note as follows:

- **Seas rising**
- **Hurricanes**
- **Melting ice**
- **Floods**

And then all will form a new type of landscape.

N: Is this good?

A: Yes, it must happen in England, London, Jersey, N. Ireland and N. Spain

N: Anything else?

A: Yes, clarification will come soon through Pegasis.

N: Pegasis? I do not understand, please clarify?

A: Energy for you to work with soon

N: Please tell me a little about this energy?

A: Well it is pure and good and knows what is right for the planet and what is wrong.

N: : Anything else?

A: No, not today,

N: I give thanks for all information received to date.

Salamander Pure Essence

Time 2am – Information Received

Salamander, salamander, salamander

Thought in my mind, got up and wrote. Earth gipsy.

N: What is a salamander? Please clarify?

A: You are like same.

N: Please clarify and explain as I do not know what a salamander is?

A: A rover, roving the earth and gaining knowledge.

N: Please clarify and elaborate?

A: Knowledge of existence from one era to another

N: Anything else please?

A: Yes, to know that all salamanders are of pure essence and knowledge exists. Must draw on it at all times while on earth.

N: Anything else?

A: Yes, read the book Whitebrotherhood P 55 N: B. (I was guided to book and page with message as follows:

'The way of the sun Angelic kingdoms salamanders solar body i.e. sun body. Work under the great solar lords, necessary in creation and in evolution of life, in etheric and physical matter. Man must go back to the real, true way of life, working together with the angels and etheric kingdoms. Life will become richer and will see that all is eternal life. Help by good thoughts and true love i.e. power is in pure thought and in the moment. All creation at etheric level of life is very receptive to the quality love to the quality of thought.'

This is why brotherhood is endeavouring to instil good brotherly thought into man's mind. God be with you all, see with your higher mind and the waving gold of cornfields, thank thee for the blessing.

Reiki Energy:

N: Do you have a message for me?

A: We wish to discuss Reiki.

N: Reiki symbol shown to me.

A: Reiki will shift many people on to a new level of consciousness, in the very near future. Do you understand?

N: Yes

A: Now is the time to OOOOOOOOOOOOOOO form circles on earth 2000. Is it very urgent? Prayer circles, enlightening circles, all positive power, meditation circles, inspirational writers' circles etc.

N: Why please?

A: Because during the last century all people believed in the physical and material side of life. Now, in the present day, the highly evolved and not so highly evolved are seeking something outside of that existence. By this we mean existing on earth as animals. People have a higher intelligence quota, and it has not been totally used in the past. So let us now allow this side of growth in the present time. The world needs, what help, help, help.

N: What kind of help?

A: Healers to put back:

Love to planet

To people who live on it

To seas (oceans) fish

Animals on global level

N: Ok yes, anything else?

A: No.

N: I do appreciate this advice, thanks.

A: Like a spring all Reiki will bounce back with the power of good universal energy. More information tomorrow.

N: Much gratitude as always for this valuable information.

Thought Process and Vibration help with Our Salvation

Year 2001 - Affirmations

"Power is in pure thought and in the moment"

A: Our message for you today Nollaig.

N: Go ahead please what is the message?

A: On disease, that of 'Foot and Mouth', to know that it will get worse affecting France, Ireland North and the South of England. This is going to slow up travel, combined with fuel.

N: Why is this happening?

A: To make people stop the abuse of animals. It's happening all the time, killing, eating and feeding incorrectly. When animals suffer, people suffer. Horses also need protection from mankind, they are hard working and they are and always at hand to help mankind.

N: Why England please?

A: It is the country that is leading the world in many ways. People look up to England but it is losing power now that Europe is united.

N: Is E.E.C. a good thing, yes or no?

A: Yes and no, by yes we mean growth and advancement, internet, computers, travel, communications etc. By no we mean evolvement in people slowing down too much corruption in Europe. Greed and conflict must stop soon. Things will happen to make people take note and step back. Now is the time for growth in spirit as materialism is outgrowing the spirit in some and this cannot happen at this particular time on earth.

N: Anything else today?

A: Refugees, Asylum seekers… (See poem 'The Berlin Wall')

N: Should they be allowed into Britain and Ireland?

A: Yes, suffering at the hands of madmen, corruption again here. This always comes out of power, guns, dictatorship and that is how it is. These people have nothing and need to be cared for. They are the victims, some good, and some bad. As in general never look up to or down upon any individual. All on journeys, above all do not judge. It is not your job. Do you understand this very important information my child?

N: Yes, as always I give thanks, anything else?

A: No, go now in peace, open your heart. Listen and evolve, be cured of all bad thoughts, all negativity and ill feelings that you hold on to as this will only stifle growth and we need you to grow even more form here in order to carry out this great work. Rise above in the eight meditations and the figure 8. You have come a long way and will need to keep rising above in pure positive thought power, as we pass on our affirmation 'power is in pure thought and in the moment'. A little more on asylum seekers my child. They are here for a reason.

N: What reason please?

A: To teach people about poverty, greed etc. It is not their fault, to be in this position you will learn much from these people as suffering knowledge re: dictatorship and much, much more. They must be helped now as the world is unfairly divided. Support them in healing/relaxation and drawing out knowledge from their past, their countries' feelings, why they are here etc.

N: I give thanks.

Today we would like to discuss the **Art of Listening**

A: We the Atlantians' of the Christ essence would like to share with you on listening. You are tuned into the energy field and raising your own vibration to connect with us. You must give yourself time to listen - stop - tune into the higher frequency. Try it, it works, do not let the logical mind answer. As this is old now, vibrations on earth have already risen. You are in tune, but not giving the self time to listen. It is an art that must be achieved to conquer, to counsel and be. Understand this message Nollaig?

N: Yes, I do.

A: Now we wish to thank you for your great work and dedication, we work well with you and through you as a channel. Now, today's message or lesson is to know that all is in order for change. People are not in line yet. But the energy is speeding up and getting faster and more urgent so it is only a matter of time and people do not have much time to spare. Must come in line with a plan for the planet or there will be no planet to live on. Do you understand?

N: Yes.

People

A: We will continue on the topic of people. All people are equal; they are the same in needs and wants, etc. Now people do not see it that way. Greed is evil and taking over it is not the work of God. Be simple in needs, enough for all, but it's a sense of security to want much and look down on those who do not possess material goods sometimes. These people have more spiritual wealth and that is what is needed now, not material wealth. It is possible to have both with the correct attitude. You will have same one day, but priorities are in order and you can fit in. Teach this please.

N: I will do. Anything else, please?

A: We feel that things are on the mend up, by that we mean that people are becoming more aware of the true self. Your mission will be easier than at first thought, understand?

N: Clarify please for me.

A: People are looking to the self without realising it, on a universal level. It will be automatic, as one consciousness, universal consciousness.

N: I give thanks for this great knowledge received. Anything else please?

A: Yes, to know that we are very happy with your progress, take vitamins, next week walk and swim, work on blue light with throat area sends the light to all on earth. Do not get caught up in any issues not yours, work on self now, great chance here in Spain before moving in March. Get in touch with Dr. Ana Cisneros re: meditation record the 8 meditation It will be of great benefit to get out the message re: channelling. (See 8th Meditation - page 159)

N: Yes it would, anything else? I give thanks.

A: You will transform on a very high level so only those that have done work on themselves will qualify, qualify or be ready if you know what we are saying.

N: No please clarify now please.

A: Well, all are on journeys, some evolved highly, some on lower frequency, and some just becoming aware of their task or mission. It is very important that you do not waste your energy, we know who to send. Just prepare, energise self, promote a little and wait. You will be surprised and well rewarded if you listen to us, ok?

N: Yes. Anything else?

A: Anything else, do you understand about being ready?

N: Yes, but what will I do if I feel somebody is ready?

A: You will know through us, trust now please.

N: Anything else?

A: Yes.

N: What, please?

A: To know that all matters of the heart are being taken into account now and when the time is correct there will be an overflowing of power and healing and the vibrations will then rise. Be ready, be in the light, be positive and feel the vibrations.

N: Anything else?

A: Yes

N: Go ahead please.

A: Well the flow is getting more consistent and that is good for you but you must get cracking on meditation, preparing for the mighty surge in the outpouring of hearts as all people are feeling the pain and suffering, but are not highlighting things, brushing under the carpet and avoiding same. That is how it is now in the world but it will change soon.

Negative and Positive Thought Process

A: Today we greet you once again and as always we are your Atlantian friends bringing much knowledge lost over time and thinking in a negative way, over the ages. We are always at hand to help you on this very important mission, putting others on their paths, without diverting from yours. You must keep straight on it. Single-minded and charismatic in all deeds, keep in purity and of course at all times those who are not in truth are not ready. You must keep in total truth, do not look up to or down upon as we taught you before. Understand my child?

N: Yes.

A: Very well, we will continue. You are doing good work but must stop thinking to reserve energy. In order for us to contact you energies need to be high. We advise good diet, rest, exercise and relaxation, meditation, reiki, colour healing, horse riding and more. Also to know that in the near future you will deliver our messages by means of communications, radio, schools, papers, TV and more.

N: What messages please?

A: About mankind and its sufferings now. It has to happen to quieten same and good will overcome evil. Understand?

N: Yes

A: All is coming to a head now, wars, all sadness will be cleansed from the earth soon.

N: How please?

A: Planet will dictate in its own way. Now about America, it will get worse before it gets better. Much suffering to come to her and her people. A type of a karma dept. Do you understand?

N: Please clarify.

A: By this we mean owing to other countries they had it good for a long time. Now is the time to pay back and the people will suffer? Good as well as bad.

N: Why the good please explain?

A: Balance in both worlds – in both energies understand? Physical and spiritual. That is all for today go in peace and light.

N: I give thanks for information received.

New Golden Age

A: Today we wish to speak a little on the New Golden Age. To know that all is good in the spirit world and the New Age is coming about sooner rather than later.

N: What do you mean please?

A: Corruption is bad and it must stop now. Trouble in the Arab world could badly affect the western part of the world on restriction on travel re: oil in the coming years.

N: Santorini Island in Greece. Please tell me a bit about it?

A: Santorini is very sacred, lost to mankind and the planet by volcanic activity, millions of years ago, under the sea, as sea will always rise and old cities are lost forever.

N: Who lived on the island?

A: Greek Gods and the like.

N: Are you connected please?

A: Directly no, but connected. You must know that you will communicate to all people that are ready in Ireland and other areas and we will write and speak through you. As you are, through us a channel of a new era, linking The New Era with old knowledge lost.

N: Much gratitude for information received.

Shock Treatment

A: Our message to you today, my fair one, is simply… that all in the spirit world are sad, and want to help, but cannot as mankind is not listening to us now, but they will when shock treatment comes.

N: When?

A: Near future

N: What kind of shock treatment please?

A: Well loss of the material world as it was and a new awakening is about to happen and it will lift mankind to a new level of existence. As evil is in control and this is not going to win. The planet will sort that out as it must to exist in this type of environment. God warns through the planet. Understand?

N: Yes. I give thanks for this valuable information for mankind and I will deliver same.

A: Again we wish to refer to mankind that the time is near for mankind to listen, you are involved with the aftermath and building Nollaig.

N: Aftermath. What do you mean please?

A: By this we mean troubled land, people and things. Your area is to bring spirit between now and 2012 in mankind, to man himself. There is much work to do on earth cleansing between now and 2012 - good from evil.

N: How please?

A: By means of planetary intersession well, as we have stated many times seas will raise, ice will melt with lots of snow and wind and all that is part of clearing. People will die. England, France and USA.

N: Anything else please. Will there be war?

A: Yes confined to Afghanistan, to east, Middle East for a long time.

N: What will happen to America?

A: People will suffer by means of lack and coping with little. More attacks possible Whitehouse perhaps. England is in danger of attack. You are doing good work but must stop thinking to reserve energy. In order for us to contact you your energies need to be high.

N: Yes, will do this every day.

Purity

N: What is your message today please my Atlantian friends?

A: Your Atlantian friends wish to share with you the essence of purity.

N: What is purity?

A: Well, my fair one, it takes working at. Purity in thought form must be achieved at this time on the planet, purity in thought form will automatically uplift the vibration of the planet in numbers getting together in pure thought only. 'Power is in pure thought and in the moment' say every day. And it will draw purity to us, ok? (Use this affirmation to bring in pure energy).

N: Yes I understand and give thanks for that.

A: Purity is the essence of Atlantis; it is the goodness in the individual that must be brought out now. There is an urgency about this. Purity in the self, the ego out the Godly side in only, always aspire to this Nollaig. You must stay on that route or path now. All negative patterns are gone forever, understand?

N: Yes I do, will try harder…well.

A: Purity is our essence, we cannot work through any other energy, other energy all round, but this is possible to raise it through. You Nollaig…..with our help……

N: Was I an Atlantian at one time?

A: Yes.

N: What was my name? Please clarify was I an Atlantian once?

A: Yes, name not important as ego related.

N: Are you of the Christ essence?

A: Yes, all is well now you are us and we are you and know that you are protected now and always, in the spirit and physical, be alert in truth, purity is very important on your path.

N: Any tips please?

A: It will work; we are working with you to draw correct energy much needed in Torrevieja in Spain.

N: Ok yes I give thanks and I agree this is a very corrupt area in South Eastern Spain.

2000 - 2010

A: Once again we wish to refer to the planet. Corruption on all levels must stop in this decade: 2000- 2010

- **Governments**
- **Greed**
- **Environmental issues**

That is basically it, England, USA and Russia involved.

N: Are we talking about war?

A: Governments must be highlighted in this decade, people running countries hiding issues, ammunition, bombs and nuclear weapons must be highlighted by United Nations. If doing their job properly, if not vulnerable to corruption. Wait, watch and see with your own eye, the level of corrupt thinking in the world.

Power

Power, power, power and ego that is basically the size of it and the way the world is. It must stop now in order to get things back on track before it is too late.

N: How long do we have please?

A: This decade is very important to put in order. Now is the time to work on people and make them see their own power and truth. It is the only way forward. As always, all are equal on earth. Own power to all and no dependency when at all possible, to all earthly being, missions and journeys etc, accountable not only to man, but to divine source that is greater higher and more powerful that all planets put together. Understand my child?

A: Yes that is very clear, I give thanks.

Own Divinity

A: The time is running out for the planet, all must be in line for the new energy. All must shift as planets are changing and people are STUCK. People need more love (see poem titled 'Love') they need to go within and recognise the lost part of their very being and re-connect.

Stop looking outside of themselves for enjoyment. Now is the time to connect with the God within. Governments want power, not Godly but the human type. Saddam Hussein is the same, all bad must change the war with Iraq, this time will succeed but sadly many will die. Chemicals, guns etc are bad. Evil men killing themselves and their people. This is not the way God planned. Give man power and he is a danger to himself and others. Animals still suffering.

Enough of that now, you must be more vigilant with people in travels. We are Atlantians' crystal and light energy. Of the Christ essence, sending love and light and energy to all situations. Listen now, focus is very important, God will deliver people's messages re:

- Paths
- Planetary information
- Own healing journey
- Healing of others

Sometimes information for them, sometimes not, but all good information is coming your way now we will deliver, through you, the new golden age. With much information soon.

N: Gratitude as always, Nollaig.

Christ Consciousness

A: Thank you for your co-operation and information about to be recorded today our fair earthly channel, we will now precede. Our message for today is to know that in time all will fit into place. As above so below. The time is near now for change and change is necessary in order to go forward. This is the wisdom speaking from the Atlantian force of the Christ essence. No other. Always working to enhance the Christ essence. There are many different types of essences floating at his important time on earth.

Some good, some bad, some ok. Some need purification to be worked upon, as aspiring towards the light. Free will and free choice is very important on your path. Do not mix these two very important things. People need to be ready, not rushed in anyway. If not ready, energy is lost wasted on explaining. All must come into own power in truth. Understand?

N: Yes, anything else?

A: All is well; all is quiet waiting for planets to take enlightenment. By that we mean in all balance. Earth must vibrate at a higher level soon. It is as simple as that. It cannot be stuck in the new age Aquarius. Strength in women is paramount in the new era and the gentle feminine side of man to come to the core. All people must take back their own power. All beings on earth are in control of their own power, but they give it away.

We would now like to continue on the lesson state of mankind.

Lesson State of Mankind

A: You must learn that all beings are different in a sense, where they are coming from, the lesson state etc. Not bad, just on a journey influenced by the outer more materialistic world and need to strike the balance their inner/outer for harmony. You my child have got to this stage, but must keep working on the self, as perfection is the art of correction on the self on an ongoing basis, not all have reached this stage, other people they must learn this. Is that clear?

N: Yes

A: You must always ask for information, it is part of knowledge, and knowledge is growth.

N: Why did you choose me?

A: Your soul is at the evolved state that can be contacted.

N: With whom do I speak?

A: Jacob - assistant to the seven steps of evolvement.

N: I give thanks for the information received.

Confirmation of My Mission

A: Today we would like to confirm that you will, through the Golden Age, deliver information on people's messages.

Re Paths
Re Planetary information
Re Own healing journey and healing of others.
All will come together in the near future. Circles channelling from above on a global level. Healing, cleansing, the weather etc.
We are getting rid of negative energies.
People will be drawn to light, correct path and enlightenment faster or they will be shocked into it.

N: How please?

A: Will not reveal now.

N: Much gratitude, with respect to your decision.

A: We can relay information on world issues. All will come to a head in the near future and will startle the world. The planet will act, northern waters, ice, storms, death of animals and some people in countries, England, Russia, USA, and Islamic countries. This is inevitable.

N: What will happen please?

A: Oceans will rise as we have stated - winds, mini and larger earthquakes. It will be worldwide. Oil will rise and this will have a great effect on the western economy. A slow-down on trade etc. The Arab States could badly affect the western part of the world. Restrictions on travel and oil as already stated.

N: Anything else please?

A: Yes, Humanism will be the dominant feature of the coming Aquarian age. We are in a time of transition. Materialism is now history. God divinity in all the source of all. That is how it is and will be in this era. You will teach this in many different ways with our assistance, using colour, crystal energy and reiki etc. When correct people connect, you will know. They are ready for this life.

N: Much gratitude as always for information to share with mankind.

Atlantians in relation to Spiritual Aspects of Man:

N: Hello do you have a message for me please?

A: Yes

N: Go ahead please, thanks in advance for information.

A: Well you already know much about the Atlantians from books. It is important to know that they lived and worked hard for mankind and evolvement of the people and the planet. You will teach from this prospective Nollaig when the time is correct, they were the purest, finest and most disciplined race that ever existed in the whole history of mankind. Do you understand?

N: Yes, but please clarify, in what way?

A: In all ways and on all levels. Now today's people mainly live in the physical and forget about the spiritual aspects of man that is the Godly part, that is the soul, spirit etc, it is the part of you that we are able to contact now Nollaig. Your spirit allows us to communicate, openness is important. Freedom from all earthly bondage and material goods will come again when you have learned how to cope and not to miss the same.

Thought Process and Vibration

A: Today we wish to discuss thought process and vibration. Now you must remain in pure thought open and creative as new thoughts will come more quickly from now on, on a faster vibration. Travel to sacred places when possible. Be in the light, meditate, mix with people by all means, but you must know and learn that most people hold grudges, jealousy, even healers are on paths and live in a commercial world and some are stuck. You Nollaig have a very important mission to play in the transformation process and must not let negative thinking get in the way at any time. Understand?

N: Yes I do.

A: Very well then, we will continue. You must stop when a negative thought comes - transform it. For example, if you do not like a person. Find the light, do not criticise under any circumstances, it is not in our vibration and on a lower vibration. We cannot reach your vibration if you go to that level.

Do not ever say a bad word about a person. Just salute, enlighten, and move away as some people caught up in hurts, jealousy etc reflects in lives on the outside.

You will teach how to love, enlighten and raise above all matters in the material world, linking spirit to matter we can reach you at this point. Is that clear my fair one?

N: Yes.

A: We will show unconditional love, forgiveness through you.

N: Thank you for your guidance. I have a question, I am sitting here at Tarifa, southern Spain, looking across at Africa, and I would like information on this area please?

A: Tarifa was a famous trading port for all – slaves, fishing, people and silks. The gateway and lookout for Europe and Africa.

N: The castle on the hill, who built it please?

A: Romans/bunkers for protection of the European Empire from the outside world. Tarifa energy is good and cleansing for mankind. You will write much information soon on Atlantians and know much of lifestyles, habits and more.

Important message

A: God is all and to know that all is in the hands of God. God is all and that is what is important now, not man but God. Godly thinking, Godly doing, and Godly care etc. It is important to know that we are descendants of the Godly energy and in direct contact with earthly beings like you. Earthly beings have much ability to shift negative energy now. Only those that are ready we stress energy for now. All will suddenly fit into place at your level and you will help many lost souls, searches if you like. Searches that are ready to evolve this time and evolve they will, through your help in evolvement of mankind and children at this time are under too much influence, not Godly, commercialism is the ruination of mankind.

N: Is that all for today?

A: Yes.

N: Much gratitude as always for the information received.

Cordoba, Spain

Our message for you today is to visit Cordoba in Spain, a sacred place for all. The world should look saintly as in old times. Saints are of great importance and linked to God. There are many levels of evolvement in the spirit world. The higher one evolves on earth, the greater the work rewards etc. in the spirit life. Spirit life is orderly, as we are always. We like things in order, not confused as in the physical world. When man takes control of the Self, then the world will be better. Now you will know that all is in the now, as highly evolved souls will be drawn to you. All people in all religions have a soul and this is what is important, unconditional love, soul acknowledgement be it Muslim, Christian, Jew, Hindu etc. This is urgent to put them on correct paths. This is your mission. The rest is up to us. This is very important.

N: Anything else for today?

A: Yes, soon the world will change.

N: How please?

A: Depression if you like to slow down mankind and take all back to a basic type of living.

We wish to inform you today that you will write much information on the topic of change regarding the planet. You will touch the youth with channelled information. As the younger generation is more highly evolved, it is easier to connect regarding negative patterns. As others are stuck in habit and take much energy, they will come to you through you and we will work well. This is your mission, a great communicator in circles, clear the way in healing and cleansing.

N: Is that all the information for today?

A: Yes, my child.

N: I give thanks.

A: Today we would like to discuss Spain within Europe. We warn that things are changing on a material level. By that we mean that materialism is taking over now, spirituality is dying in Spain - this was never the case and Europe is to blame. Things will get very bad in Europe, starting with the oil. The oil will rise because of war in Middle East, this has to happen and it will. Things will slow down, especially the dollar.

N: Clarification please?

A: By the dollar we mean money, war in a word. (a) the oil has control of the west, (b) the euro has control of the people. And trade, England v Europe and Africa in a trade war.

N: Will England join in the euro please?

A: No, not for a long time as Europe depends on them. The situation is dollar v sterling v euro in time as we stated earlier people will pay, and loss of homes to banks, travel re: lack of oil. Materialism is being brought to the surface when people recognise God and not the self, they will win more trouble coming to Russia, Middle East and America getting bad now and it could spread to west America and England, having a knock-on effect on Europe.

Love

A: Our message to you Nollaig is one of love in all that you do in all that matters and in all dealings. In all ways in all people, love is the only way forward, much lacking in the world today. Now we want to talk about mankind, you will learn in time that all mankind is the same in many, many ways, no difference in colour, creed, religion and more.

N: What more?

A: Personality, it is ego related, and this time is about being whole on a collective level, understand?

N: Yes and no, clarifications?

A: By being whole as a universe, not the whole body which is part of this. Now we are a body in light, you are a body in matter. Hold on to this thought and we will proceed.

The matter of physical body is part of that universe, all that exists around on an energy level, this is how reiki works. The spiritual aspect of the matter body can be accessed through this energy quite easily when the vibration is lifted and this needs to be worked upon every day by means of prayer, diet, colour, healing, reiki and more.

N: What more?

A: That of music, dance, poetry, all is possible now as time is speeding up. You will know as time goes on you will feel from people the change, it is prominent. Understand?

N: Yes

Love poem

All in the spirit world feel the
pain and sadness of humanities suffering
on earth, but love is lacking
and love is the only way forward.
Love is transformation...
Love will heal...
Love will conquer...
and love will seal, link, uplift,
enlighten or whatever
phrase you need to use...
Love is all...
Love is lacking on earth
and now is the time to
find love in the heart...
so remember...
unconditional love
to the self,
to the planet,
and to
all
mankind

Nollaig
Atlantis

A Time to Explore
Would you like to know more?

Year 2002 –The London Thames Barrier

A: Today we would like to speak a little information about us and warning that London is in danger regarding The Thames Barrier. We worked hard on the land, we minded crystals on a continent of purity - more on that later. Next we would like to refer to matters on a global level - much water will rise - ice is melting quickly now and very strong winds to come in the future. London under much water in the coming years and The Thames in trouble. This is a time of great change and people are not in line yet, but the energy is speeding up as we speak, it is getting faster and more urgent, so it is only a matter of time to spare. People must come in line for the planet or there will be no planet to live on as discussed earlier, this is a very important issue in this decade and we may refer to reputably. As we have said 'all people are equal and they are the same, same wants and needs'. People do not see it that way. Greed is evil and it is taking over it is not the work of God. Be simple in needs. Enough for all but it's a sense of security to want much and look down on those who do not process material goods. These people have more spiritual wealth and that is what is important and needed at this time on earth, not just material wealth. It is possible to have both with the correct attitude.

N: I give thanks for this very important information.

Communication of the Spirit compared with Physical Communication

A: At the beginning of this earthly year, you must know that the time is near when all men will know truths. You feel this when one lies. It is an instant knowing when there is no truth. Truth is paramount on your path now. Truth is the essence of purity and purity is truth in all matters, coupled with love, is that clear?

N: Yes.

A: Very well, we will continue, when all men know own truths, the evolvement will take place on a collective level. It is slow as individual truths are awakening we must wait and wait we will, understand?

N: Yes I do.

Communication on the Spiritual Plane

A: Now next you must learn the art of communication on the spiritual plane, it is very deep and much different from the art of communication on the physical plane. As the art of communication on the spiritual is only for a chosen few who are ready and who have the purity and the ability to transform and to communicate this information to those that are ready on the physical plane.

N: How will I know?

A: Those that are ready will find you in a miraculous way. You must keep sowing seeds and be as it is in being still that we can connect with you on a purer vibration and a clearer note. Communication of the spirit is a very worthy mission on earth for the chosen few. You will put many souls on their paths soon: We once again are your Atlantian guides this time round, on this very important mission on earth.

N: Please tell me something about yourselves?

A: We are highly evolved, much wisdom, much loss, much love for mankind and transformation: We are all united in this mission:

N: Can I have your name please?

A: St Germain.

N: Anything Else?

A: Yes - you must feel the energy of those around you and rise above; most are still stuck in ego and have not mastered the physical plane yet, but will be awakened soon: You will help in this awakening. Be in own power now.

N: I give thanks for information received.

Tolerance

A: Our message for today is tolerance for all people on earth. Some talk - some boast - some cry - some shout - some sing and some control- some are timid. All are in the physical body and all are limited, at their stage of evolution: This is the important lesson today my child. Raise them up to enlightenment; it is possible at this time in the ascension process.

Love

A: Now we wish to talk on the topic of love. Love is all. Only love on our vibration, only love in and love out as love is the answer as in the poem (see poem page). Love is all; we can only communicate in pure thought and love. This is very difficult to achieve on earth, but possible. Work on it all the time please, keep on the light, we are helping in this very big earthly mission.

School of Light

A: You must know that in the spirit world things change in favour of the earth planet and all that is, that is how it is and always will be. Things are not always as they seem. People are not always as they appear. Get to the truth of the matter as we said before and cut the bullshit in all and you will have truth. This is basic and people will understand our expression: People are not in truth, but some are aspiring to it, few are in total truth and the time is near when men will know own truth, on all levels not just on the material plane. Understand?

N: I need clarification on 'some in truth'.

A: Well some are on the way to own truth but held back by circumstances, fear, partners etc. But few are in truth totally. This we stress needs to be worked on every day and every minute of every day as in perfection, 'which is the art of correction on the self on an ongoing basis', say this affirmation to yourself now. You will learn about growth on many levels. As in the spirit world beings are still evolving, faster than on the material level in the schools of light here. It is possible to evolve on earth at this very important time of listening. As we said 'most are not', but opportunity will come again later in the schools of light, if not on the earth plane. Now you must protect yourself always.

Europe

A: Today we send much love and light, always light to this great work, much needed on the planet today. We watch over you and we have very good vision for the future. It is more difficult now for you. Now is the time for change, on a global level and the euro. It will be good for countries concerned, as it will arouse competition which is always good. Travel will be good, cheap for a time. Openness in growth etc but be warned - it will not last.

N: Why please?

A: Corruption will set in - leadership, as corrupt people are involved with this bank and that is how it is. Corruption in the leaders in Europe and this will lead the dollar and euro into trouble, but the world is still not listening. Property will drop drastically all over Europe. Banks will repossess same, leaving some homeless. This is depressing but part of the change; wars will start among Europeans over silly things, out of frustration with the dollar v the euro. You must warn of this when the time is correct. The planet is not happy now, when ice melts, floods will rise seas and do much damage. England in danger, the sterling will suffer, as greed is there. Prestige is over for England as it will hit dark times, this is a warning for the future.

N: Will it affect Ireland please?

A: A little of course and Spain re: the slow down of corruption:

Drugs

A: The positive side of this on corruption is smuggling of drugs will slow down and stop. The price must be paid soon as it's the ruination of mankind. Mankind must listen now, still not listening. This is the vision for the future. You will be a great communicator in time my child, but you must learn to balance the physical and spiritual self in this work, it is of great importance. It is important to know that we are now living in a very important time of change. This is an exciting time for all souls. The Aquarian age being a sign of group consciousness of each individual who recognises his separateness in truth. This age will be about connecting more with humanism. People are searching now and beginning to take back their own inner power as dictatorship is crumbling as we speak and it is not working in this time of transformation: You must be in grace now to deliver our information and to know that this is time of change. There are many lessons coming quickly re: conflict and more.

Trust and Lesson State with Free Will

A: Our message for today is one of trust ... Trust is very important in the physical world. Trust in our source of the Christ Essence. You will learn in time that all changes in the spirit world are as in the material world but on a different level.

N: Clarification please?

A: Change in the sense of free will and free choice. No dominance from the spiritual world, more to the highest good and the soul to the divinity of the soul. Without interfering with the free will, on the soul's journey. Lesson state comes in here. Souls learn and grow from lessons, you have experienced this. Repentance is very important to all souls, the recognition of the lessons. Understand now my child?

N: Yes, in gratitude for your patience in explaining to me and teaching from this angle.

A: Light can be dimmed by individuals if you do not always protect, manipulation is the enemy here. Sit alone when possible, do not be pushed into anything as the free choice and free will is very important at this time in evolution.

Meditation

A: Meditation is the most important of all for you now, all will be well. The planet is changing. Quickly the ice age is returning and help is needed for all animals, fish, birds etc. You will help here in the circles of light with those who are at the correct evolved stage for this great work.

They will be well rewarded on the next level. Healing is needed and you will form groups of healers with the same intention.

N: I give thanks for this enlightening information:

Rise above Conflict

A: You must always rise above conflict and teach in this way, openness in grace is very important; people are aspiring to this now. Others are still learning and it takes time to adapt to rising above conflict. As you will always meet it. It is the cause of many souls being stuck and it must be worked upon at this time. Our message for today is to know that in time all will fit into place. As above, so below. The time is near for change as we refer to so many times in our writings and change is necessary to go forward in this decade and beyond 2000 – 2010. You will one day teach our teachings.

N: What are your teachings please?

A: Teaching of the ascended masters, we will communicate through you when you are ready. The ascended master teachings are very powerful and are urgent for all those on the ascension path, All people need to be in their own truth now and pure love.

Seven Steps

- All humankind needs to search for God within (the spark) that is no one step.
- Perfection. This has to be worked on in the master plan (perfection is the art of correction on the self on an ongoing basis).
- Letting go of the power ego related stuff. This is very important now, urgency about co-operation and non individualisation.
- Nonjudgmental as it lowers vibration.
- Is that of sorrow for wrong doings and to recognise and repent? To know that hurts are felt in our world of spirit on a very deep level.
- Grace - be in grace, in own space and gracefully in the now. Grace is the way to other heart centre in unconditional love. It is in being in grace that many blessings are bestowed on you from us. Be in grace, be in love, be centred and you will feel the power of Atlantis.
- Simplicity - is pure in its essence. No frills, falsity, by that we mean people trying to be something other than who they are. Know the self. Whatever I am be that, whatever I do be true. Be honest in fact straightforwardly acted. Be nobody else but you. Say this affirmation often.

Repentance

A: When one repents and feels sorrow for whatever it may be. All other things are cancelled, sorrow then forgiveness is automatic. With the free will and free choice sorrow has to come first. Before the forgiveness takes place, mankind has a great chance now, we are at hand to help but we need the co-operation on the earthly level to send us the energy. We are at hand to help but we need the co-operation on earthly level and send us the energy for the world's wrong doings. This is the important lesson for today Nollaig, understand?

N: Yes, I give thanks for this wonderful wisdom helping mankind at this time.

A: Simplicity is refreshing. It is a breath of fresh air for those to feel the energy.

N: I woke up and started to print, using my finger in the air, the word was Verona: Intuitively knew it was Italy. Looked up the map first thing next morning and found it near Venice.

Verona

A: Danger is coming in the future. Danger to people in this city, in the form of nuclear gas from East a possibility.

N: Could this be prevented please?

A: Yes and no. The world leaders are not taking correct steps and people will suffer. Fallout to France, Austria, Eastern States, Northern Spain and England.

Verona is targeted for this type of attack because of location to Europe.

Verona will fight back and bring Europe on board with NATO.

N: Will this lead to war?

A: Not immediately but possible. Verona is corrupt with Mafia.

N : I give thanks for information received.

A: We wish to greet you today in love combined with sacredness in the name of God. See the divinity in all. Now you will learn that sacredness in all things is the ultimate in all that one does, all that one has and all that one knows. It is all in the moment, we are all in the light. All this is now and only now. Put your power into the now. Use this affirmation always. Be in the Now. You are connected with spirit and growing in knowledge. Light to the world, in the now.

N: I give thanks.

AFFIRMATION "PUT YOUR POWER INTO THE NOW"

Christ Essence

September 2002

N: Do you have a message for me please?

A: Yes

N: Go ahead please.

A: You must know that all will be revealed soon, all will be made known through you through us and from us, is that clear?

N: Yes. When please?

A: Soon.

N: How?

A: By means of communication of voice to the world. The time is right now to share with others and shift, get them to revert back to God, God is all. They must know this now and recognise God in themselves, firstly and insist in others. Secondy, money is not God but the commercial world (internet etc) can be bad, evil and corrupt all coming to a head now. Many things highlighted soon, many, many things to be highlighted through you by us very soon.

Spain is in this category you will receive much information in all of Spain, get back to Ireland takes notes ref radio and communicate Nollaig, you must do this by the end of year, understand?

N: Yes I will do this.

The Order of Melchizedek

N: The order of Melchizedek is it of Christ essence?

A: Yes, it is a sacred order in the world. An energy coming in to help with the evolved state of being… and the planet, the order of Melchizedek will help with the heart centre in the truth. But the truth when self realised is automatic, understand Nollaig?

N: Yes, I need a little clarification.

A: The order of Melchizedek is of the purest essence and not to be taken lightly by anyone, it is sacred and it is old. It is opening the souls to the sacred energy that lies within the heart there but lost through negative thoughts and possible now to be awakened, understand?

N: Yes, was I initiated into this?

A: Yes, you were same a priestess in those times in Egypt and Atlantis, energy is all around you now, you will work with this energy later the pure energy of Atlantis.

N: Anymore information on this please?

A: Well Atlantis was the purest, civilisation on earth, purer that the Egyptians and Lumarians.

N: Any more information for me to pass on please?

A: Yes, Atlantis is the energy coming through now, like the Christ born two thousand years ago, Atlantis is the energy to evolve and to shift the Godly earth, but people have to rise to this vibration, all are held on a lower vibration. And all must know of us, do you understand? Now you will make statements when time is near, we will inform, patience is neccessary and send out the light to Bush, Gadaffi, Saddam, Arafat. Nollaig we would like you to transfer our message to the media with our guidance soon.

N: How?

A: Write and say and know that is important to share with the world.

N: Is that all?

A: For now yes.

A Time to Let Go and Just Be

The Ascension Process

A: All are on routes – all are on journeys. All eventually will have to come in line and work up to the ascension holding themselves back by fear. Fear must go now, help is at hand, joy to all happiness waits. Those who trust and are in truth be true to the self, this is the message for today.

Atlantis: a Lost Civilisation

A: Bringing much love and light at this time of transformation on our planet. According to the cosmic calendar of the ancient Mayan civilisation we are now in the time of transformation of matter, material. We can transform matter by introducing our soul, and then we will see more clearly what is it are that really matters. Getting on the right path, there is a plan in store for us. Know your mission in life, this is very important. Wisdom from past knowledge ancient Mayan king, was a good Politian, a good king and a good ruler.

Purity, free will and free choice is what is important now. Live it day to day and follow your true path.

Justice

A: Message for today Nollaig is one of justice.

Justice in life, justice is very important on route to ascension. Justice in life. No human being has the right to undermine or to kill, or cause damage to others, repentance on wrong doing on lesson state. It is in recognising and asking for forgiveness, that man evolves. People are defensive and not aware enough of wrong doings re: war and the US President.

It is murder on a very large scale, he is bad and knows of his wrong doings, false front in worship. No repentance, Blair is of different belief, both powerful leaders.

Saddam is evil corrupt and will answer when on next level. It is God's area to punish, not Bush, Blair or anybody? Civilians are all killed in cold blood, for what? Governments at fault. Nobody knows, it is not just.

No justice at this very low level it has to stop and stop it will.

Iraq and Saddam

A: We are your guides of the Christ essence and the Atlantian energy

We come with much love today as always now you must know that all is changing in the war from evil to dominance. Dominance in the real sense of torture still existing. The war is not over; things will get worse before getting better, understand?

N: Yes and no, please clarify, what will happen?

A: Well in Iraq is energy changing all the time, still negative still bad, still Saddam's regime are around the area it will take time to get him, this evil man and many things will happen before he is executed in the sense of corruption: To USA, to England and more, that of lies, corruption, hunger, oil strikes and more climate change. The climate is heating up in the south and drought will come. We would like to advise you of the many changes to come on the physical level. In time the world will be a different place to live, but many changes will take place before then do you understand?

N: Would like clarification on change please.

A: The change that we are referring to is one of climate, of drought and more abuse of souls in a corrupt way in Iraq is only starting and will continue for a time, America will leave soon and the real trouble will start amongst all corrupt leaders, understand?

N: Yes.

A: Saddam will carry on for a while in the background and will eventually be assassinated in time but it will take time and many lives to get him, this evil man working in greed and torture. This will have to be highlighted, America is taking praise for nothing. Not helping the starving people and the situation only power, oil will rise up, heat more heat in all southern countries will cause a global problem with water and colder climate in the north. Freezing times to come this is the climatic change and lots of information to come in the near future for you.

Inspiration and Knowledge

A: Message for today Nollaig is that of knowledge and inspiration, inspired from spirit, from the true essence of the being on a particular path, to record inspiration is to tune into the self, the soul and know that it is correct. Do you understand?

N: I understand yes but please clarify the message to me?

A: You must stop chatting, that is not in-depth and tune into the truth in all matters no small talk, it will trigger off the truth in all do not cover up for man as all are aspiring to this truth now in this special time on earth, Christ is helping, his essence will bring in the light and the truth in all. You will teach this, guided from above. Now you must meditate, teach meditation, teach Reiki and use crystal, all of this knowledge is freely available to you now. Herbs, colour and more.

N: What more?

A: That of counselling, understanding and listening to us a true channellor, do not let others interfere or put you off. All are on paths and at the different levels. Now you will teach on your return to Ireland and write by the sea. Now to power. Power is purity in thought. Repentance and love brings light to all situations, understand?

N: Yes, thank you to all for this information:

A: More to come now. That of children, children are misused as power for power, and held in much esteem through adults. How can a child know its power when parents do not? Teach from this perspective Nollaig. You will win in all situations. Win, win, win is the outcome here.

Knowledge is at hand to help, the choice is important, free will and free choice to all mankind. We the Atlantians and Mayans love our work as teachers of mankind, teachers in pure thought form and in pure Godly power through our chosen channels on earth. Keep grounded, keep in the now, keep calm, keep meditating, keep sending out the light, keep up the good work we will send the energy needed this very important mission. We will send as appropriate to you or chosen channel. All is well now.

N: Thank you for the wisdom from Atlantis.

Meditation

A: My child the lesson for today is one of meditation as in meditation we access our very true souls being understood. Our soul's being always needs acknowledgement from our physical being, when acknowledged and recognised it has more power for guidance to come through. This is very important to your work in counselling channelling and meditation. Any questions?

N: Is my soul my body?

A: No, your soul chooses many bodies and many lives on its journey to enlightenment, understand?

N: Yes I do.

A: Your soul is more important but body is secondary, it is very important in the sense that it houses the soul, understand?

N: Yes I do.

A: You in body are in the now, we are in the light, we the Atlantian civilisation know much regarding evolvement as we were the highest, most sacred and advanced race that ever lived as earthly beings and we want to teach the world of our knowledge. We made mistakes, very bad mistakes and the planet is in much danger now of repeating history. The world is bad, evil and not as intended with reference to lesson state. Enlightenment in all is very important. Greed, power and more has taken over and tilted the balance in a much negative way. We want this to change and change it will by means of war. Now there is no other way many will die, and that is how it is. You must tell the world of us soon: It is necessary for a clean up, a shake up and for some leaders to go.

N: What would you like me to say to the world?

A: You will know through us, wait a little longer for guidance, tune in every day and stay Godly in purity and in unconditional love. In time people will repent, work with repentance. It is good, humble and much needed in the corrupt way of living. Do not ever come to this level. Greed is killing many, too much and wants more, God will provide when asked to the highest good of the soul. The soul needs more spiritual guidance than material wants understand?

N: Yes I do.

A: Colour is very important on your path; you are good with this healing essence, use it combined with Reiki. This is very important and crystals hold the knowledge. Use them often, tune in and ask for our help, guidance and more.

Solitude

A: Message for today Nollaig is one of solitude alone in the self and spirit of the matter. Not getting caught up in the superficial aspects of the material life or life on the material plane, understand?

N: Yes and no, please clarify solitude in my case.

A: Solitude is very important on your path as others are on the surface talk, talk, talk and in no depth. All ok, but at this level you are different and happy in solitude, you need to mix occasionally, but remember do not mix if the feeling is not correct. Free will and free choice as always is the thing to adhere to my child and you are doing well here in keeping to the self and being social at the same time, keep it up.

Our message for today is one of torture

A: It is the lowest kind of treatment that a human being can give or receive at the hands of mad men, bad men and it is power driven. It is sad and it is going to stop in time. It will take time to change the thinking in these people bullying as they are of a different temperament than the educated ones. In time it will change it has to change but torture is the lowest vibration and not in the Christ essences understand?

N: Yes, please clarify where is it?

A: Torture is of the evil, bad of the demon, but in time it will not win when the earth's vibrations raise the vibrations of the energy does not and will not have the power to treat mankind, in this way mankind is killing mankind. We are very sad at this we will make the necessary vibrational change. It will take a bit of time to get these evil people. Send love and light and healing to these situations now not hate as we feel it is not the way.

Transformation Programme and Circles of Light

A: We the Atlantian essence, ancient Mayan and Atlantian civilisation and of the Christ essence want to inform you of our place on the transformation programme at this time on earth in as always the Christ essence. This is a wonderful time to live, when ready to evolve, as much help is at hand. Our mission in this great plan is to stall negativity by means of circles and divert the energy and to channel much needed positive energy to earth at this time to those that are ready. In bringing these light workers together we are in the transformation plan and it will be great. Anybody involved with this great plan will be greatly enhanced and rewarded on the next level. The next level is more about teaching from a more evolved state out of the earthly bondage to the physical, understand?

N: Yes, is it as you teach?

A: Yes but a lower level, the soul moves up in steps, levels, lessons learned and love, the state of unconditional love. This is very important at this very important time, this particular time as the unconditional love is all in the Atlantian essence and in the heart vibration. It is the energy for this time; no other will win only love, pure unconditional love to all. Now we are heavenly souls in much sorrow at the planet and we wish mankind would understand that material wants are of no use when put before God. Is that clear to you my child?

N: Yes.

A: Keep it that way; do not let houses, cars, materialism get in the way. Do not get caught up in this materialism. Healing centre will come in Ireland Mullaghamore through you/us, be focused and bring it into being. Set up Circles of Light, Transformation and truth linking those in self truth and unconditional love. Send light to world leaders, countries, religion and animals. Wednesday evening we will assist in this mission when correct energy is drawn together.

Peace to Soul

A: Message for today Nollaig is one of peace, peace to all through love, unconditional love. Try this: salute the divinity, offer peace to the soul's journey and be in unconditional love. Risen above all the soul will not hurt you it is the conflict between the mind and the physical influence that is the problems, understand?

N: Yes I think so, please clarify a little.

A: Well the mind is physical existence related chatting away to the interference of the soul's journey. When one acknowledges the true soul's essence the true journey and the lessons it is not in conflict it does not have to prove anything to anybody, great freedom from the material needs here the spiritual aspect of the being is very important as it is in cooperation with the soul's journey and to the highest good of the keeper, the physical, the mind can sometimes get in the way and lead the soul astray in conflict with the journey, not intentionally, do you understand?

N: Yes.

A: Above all it must recognise the soul is the physical existence on the earthly plane and also important in the physical realm. Your job Nollaig is to create the balance, the balance is what we are striving for in the figure 8 bring the issues into the heart, understand?

N: Yes I do.

A: Peace to all, out of peace comes love to uplift, out of love comes the change, transformation is possible now through love on earth, this is lacking and no peace in the souls of many, understand?

N: Yes I give thanks for all information received to date.

Transformation Programme

A: Now we want to talk about the Atlantians, we are teaching our methods through you to the world. At this time we have the knowledge lost over the centuries as evolvement brings with it many changes, some good, some bad and some just ok. Your soul was with us on a journey during the Atlantian civilisation as a monk.

N: Is this true?

A: Yes, this is true. The cross is sacred in and through you always call on this the cross the saviour of all souls in light, you will teach from this prospective we lived a pure life no influences from others all were pure in love, this needs to re-awaken in souls now love will transform many this time at this stage of evolvement.

Music

A: The message coming through is one of music.

A: Music is good for your soul, for anybody's soul, listen, feel and know the notes will take the soul to different levels of enlightenment. Music and poetry is good, all music, song writing, poetry writing and more.

Dominance

A: Set the pace, by that we mean order not dominance, difference here. Order is important in the spiritual or spirit world as free choice is allowed here and free will always. But dominance is ego related, always watch this in the physical as most problems come from here when order is installed in circles, discipline is automatic, all humans in physical need discipline to a point or at least need to discipline themselves, understand?

N: Yes.

A: Well then use order in that fashion and it will work for you/us. Now to the art of prayer/affirmations.

N: What kind please?

A: Introducing affirmations which are prayers in all circles "I am an enlightened being drawing all enlightened people to me in circles", always say this and be. Let things flow and flow they will.

The Art of Transformation

A: Atlantis lost civilisation awakening many memories now in those souls who are on that vibration Atlantis was the oldest and wisest and purest continent that ever existed is not a myth. It is true, now we want you to mention the work of crystals. Atlantians mined crystals and worked with colour healing, pottery and the land and more.

N: What more, clarification please, that of what animals?

A: Horses need energy healing affected by the negativity in the land planet. Dolphins are in much trouble now more than ever, dolphins are crying out for help as they want to help mankind but need the healing energy to allow same, understand?

N: Yes.

Teachings

A: We the Atlantian essence, ancient Mayan and Atlantian civilisation want to inform you of our place on the transformation programme at this time on earth in as always the Christ essence. This is a wonderful time to live when ready to evolve as much is help is at hand. Our mission in this great plan is to stall negativity, by means of circles and divert the energy channel much needed positive energy to earth. At this time through those that are ready in bringing these light workers together we are in the transformation plan and it will be great, anybody involved with this plan will be greatly enhanced and rewarded in or on the next level. The next level is more about teaching from a more evolved state out of the earthly bondage of the physical, understand?

N: Yes and no, how please? Is it as you teach?

A: Yes, but at a lower level the soul moves up in steps, levels re. Lessons learned and more.

N: What more?

A: That of love the state of unconditional love this is very important at this particular time as the unconditional love is all in the Atlantian essence and in the heart vibration. It is the energy for this time no other will win only love pure unconditional love to all, understand?

N: Yes.

A: Now to all heavenly souls in much sorrow at the planet, we wish mankind would understand that material wants are of no use if put before God, is that clear to you my child?

N: Yes.

A: Now to fault.

N: Go ahead please in gratitude and joy and much love, unconditional love as always.

Fault

A: Nollaig our fair one, the message for today is one fault, fault in things, fault in life, there is no fault people blame and more blame all the time, fault is in the material world not in the heart, not in unconditional love. Understand?

N: Yes.

Climate Change

A: All is in the now and in love from the light, we want to warn you of these things to come.

That of drought in the southern countries, this will be bad this summer in Spain and Africa, Iraq, Saudi, Mexico and all the southern countries. Climate is warming up at a very high rate.

Much trouble to come in Iraq re: leadership religious war and more, that of torture to those that have gone against the regime, understand?

N: No, please clarify.

A: America get their information from those and then leave them in a vulnerable state, this is not fair to those people. Protection is necessary both from England and USA. Bad leaders everywhere in religious offshoot communities, committees or organisations, understand?

N: Yes and no. A clear line of communication please.

A: Iraq is in danger of being still under the old regime that of the thinking etc will take years, understand?

N: Yes.

A: Now to other matters.

Korea will be a danger to USA and the world with weapons. They need to be addressed by United Nations or a new type of body as United Nations are not great now, in the people involved in same, understand?

N: Yes.

A: Wait and see Coreo combined with Sars is a disaster. Now to you, you will this summer teach crystals through us, you will do Atlantis workshops and incorporate our teachings/warnings, healing, colour, poetry and more.

N: What more?

A: That of our culture.

N: What was your culture please?

Atlantian Lifestyle

A: We as we have mentioned lived well, mined crystals, lived the Godly way of life near to God. We were at one time very wealthy but lost through greed and were wiped out in floods. The floods did come and some escaped to Egypt, this is true. Before the floods we were very much in tune with nature, before the greed set in. We dealt in silks, crystals, colour dies, horses and that of onyx also gold, silver but crystals were the biggest mining business of our time. We ate life force, light foods, and the sun, we worshipped the sun, in a thankful way for giving us life force and we sang and danced.

N: Water, what is the connection with water please?

A: We were surrounded by water on an island away from influence of others, a very special and pure race on to our own, others came later. In the beginning we were just Atlantians, Mayans and knowledgeable in our doings in our wisdom, wisdom near to God on earth in spiritual mode. We lost this through greed and trying to be more eventful and powerful with the help of others. We were influenced in a wrong way and drawn away from our purity. You worked with us on the continent of Atlantis.

N: What was my work please?

A: Priestess initiating others, healing and colour is in your blue print. This is all now Nollaig, go in peace my child and please tune in tomorrow as always crystal clear love.

Poem Title
'Crystal Culture'

Crystals are clear, they are very dear.
From us you will hear that they are near
The time is correct to introduce now into the energy field once more.
To those who are ready in a vibration way
That is all we have to say crystals will show the way
They will not lead you astray and you will do much work in May,
As crystals you will lay at Mullaghmore by the sea that is where we will be,
Adios my child just a little gift for your open day on culture,
Call it crystal culture if you like from Atlantis.

Atlantis

A: Title crystal culture seaweed was also used, spas were the best, that is all love and more love.

N: In much gratitude for beautiful poem received, Nollaig.

Democracy

A: Religious crazy beliefs are now out of the hands of the world leaders and mankind are fighting and killing themselves. This is bad, soon the climate will quieten many this is so and this is necessary draught earthquakes things are quickening now. Bombers in North Africa are going to hit again in England soon. England is going to be in trouble this summer. England will trigger off something within Western Europe on a monetary level causing much trouble within the E.E.C. Democracy is being threatened by a wave of suicide bombers, this will come later for now terrorism is at its highest, as we said before suicide bombers are not a good idea. Democracy is breaking down, this is true.

World Leader and Greed

A: This is a very dangerous situation to be in, governed and brought about by the world leaders and their greed, no value of humanism now. This is a dangerous world situation. People in time will adjust and revert back to God, it is the only way. All will win in the godly way once had and lost by many, this will change. In order to bring about the golden age much is needed, this is the message for today - be careful, only speak truth to those that are ready, save energy much needed for this very important mission. We the Atlantian ancient civilisation know much regarding evolution. We are now in a very important time in our calendar for events in this great plan, all old regimes are crumbling, not working as power has won. In evil ways in old times, old era but will not win in this era. Back to spirituality, is this clear? Relay to the world all that has been given soon Nollaig.

N: Yes I give thanks.

Challenge

A: Good afternoon Nollaig, as we speak to you from the 5th dimension we bring much light to you and all that you touch on the earth. Thank you for your great work and patience in this very important project. Challenge is good for the ego. As in pushing the self to the limit. One can and will grow, challenge in your work is important, Mullaghmore, Co Sligo is slowing down now a new project awaits in Spain.

N: What project please?

A: By means of workshops in various languages, German, Spanish, etc. Be open to all, at the mind body centre and to teaching Reiki combined with crystals and colours. Colour and of course the channelling this will be a big part of your future work now. We want you to be patient in communications. It will happen when the time is correct. TV, radio etc. Not ready yet (not you, the receptive side), understand?

N: Clarification please.

A: Next year will be big for you, we will start to prepare you when living in Spain, it will start there and return to Ireland projects, of a different type.

N: What type please?

A: That of creativity. Ireland is going to wake up soon to our very important messages

N: What will happen please?

A: It will be costly in Ireland fuel, coldness and the cost of living, banks and the government will not win this time. All people will gang up against them. This will happen – 5 years approx 2008/2009. Newness in thinking is necessary old regimes are materialistic and breaking down. This is so. Now you must learn that all humankind are the same in the matter of mental, physical and spiritual bodies. Ability to bring all together to the higher dimensions speaking through you. You must know that in time people will listen to you.

N: When please?

A: 2004/05 hopefully free choice as always. Mars will change things.

N: How please?

A: Mars will influence mankind's monetary system at a negative force.

N: How please?

A: Greed will come to surface in autumn. People will not like the way mankind is being treated. Understand and all will retaliate.

N: How?

A: By means of strikes. Change in lifestyle, cut backs etc. People will begin to take back their own power and will value the simple things once more but it will take time, 1 to 5 years. For this realisation to set in and all will be well. Now to other matters relating to war, war in Afghanistan, India will get rough, between the two countries it will trigger off China to intervene against America, understand?

N: No, clarification please.

A: Afghanistan/India against each other and Korea against America. North Korea will back the Indian country and this will lead to much turmoil in days to come.

N: How? Please.

A: N Korea will back India. As in trouble with Afghanistan, America is not helping with Afghanistan: America will suffer once again by means of disaster.

N: What kind please?

A: Avalanches in the ski resorts, all climate related. Ice melting and more.

N: What more please?

A: That of water rising. Water rising at a high level, the ice is rushing into rivers, seas rising and more. That of warm weather, it is causing an imbalance in people. Imbalance in the people and imbalances in the climate. In weather and in all. Climate is in danger of returning to the ice age as we have said many, many times. Ice age - bitterly cold. This is possible in the Northern Hemisphere. Canada, America, Scotland and that is how it will be in the future. More on that later. This will have to be highlighted, America taking praise for nothing, not helping the starving people and the situation only power, oil will rise up once again, heat, more heat in all southern countries will cause a global problem with water and colder climate in the north. Freezing times to come, this is the climate change and lots of information to come in the near future for you.

December 2003

A: Nollaig we would like to warn you of forthcoming events within the coming decade. It will take time to sort out good from evil; this is a big problem in the world now. Evil is rising, in all, in people, in power, in lack of love and in all mankind dealings against each other. It must stop and it will soon. Things will happen on the planet to make people stop and take note. Seas will rise, storms and floods. England will suffer and the floods will be great in France, Jersey and all will be under water in the future. Distant future understand.

N: Clarification please.

A: In time to come with planetary change global warming and seas rising, Jersey and England South will be in much trouble. Tidal waves and more, this is for the future. Now to more current matters, Saddam is finished, this regime is the start of finer things to come. It is over tumbled light will shine and the people of Iraq but they have a way to go and much help is needed by America to cleanse after this evil man it will be drawn out for a time, but it is a positive for future light. Afghanistan is bad evil, next it must be conquered and it will, North Korea could attack USA: A new government is necessary in USA in order to go forward in the new golden age and light must shine on USA, understand my child?

N: Yes and no, clarification please.

A: Bush must go soon and he will.

N: Anything else?

A: Yes you must know that time will speed up and the world is moving fast now. Change is necessary and a slowing down process, understand?

N: Yes.

A: Your work will involve much planetary healing from Ireland, this coming season from the cottage great for this work you sit and meditate and be patient my child, we have much information for you to share with the world soon and you must be ready.

Life on Earth

A: Life on earth is evolving very fast now, it needs to adjust to the new vibration and rising up is very important to people's vibrations otherwise it is difficult for them to exist on this faster vibration, when there is density all round and there is. Density is a darker vibration under manipulation and influence by media and by men, by some women, by life's challenges and by wants putting all before God and this is not the way. God is at the centre of all mankind's existence and one should recognise this very important fact. In time all will know divinity in the self, this is the very important message today Nollaig.

Atlantian Channelled Information
Would you like to know more?

2004

N: I am grateful for all this information coming through….. I enjoy working together and welcome to the earthly 2004.

A: We appreciate this gratitude and we would like to wish you much light, unconditional love and trust in us. Rising to our vibration is hard work and you need constant care and rest, rest is very important. The red flash of inspiration in the third eye was a very powerful gift for you for this decade. This year we and you through us will win in healing in communication to the world about us the Atlantians who were the most advanced race of humankind to ever exist on the planet.

We were and are pure in the Christ vibration and essence. Through mistakes of the earthly type of command and change and dominance, we lost what we achieved to date. We are trying to help with this evolutionary path of people's souls and to bring them to the vibrations required for the great change into the golden age. Do you understand?

N: Yes and no, clarification once again please.

A: What we want and require is truth… (A) in the self, (B) in all souls, this is lacking in most. Mankind must recognise truth in the self now it is the most important thing then light. It takes working at… bringing light to dark areas on earth. This is slowly happening and in time, in years to come the truth will win. You must be firm in the Atlantian name in truth and in the Christ essence in all matters relating to our wisdom, communicating through you for the world's benefit with as always free will and free choice for the souls concerned. Global warming is having a great effect now. Ice is sailing southwards and in March rivers will rise and all will flood, this is the warning today and hot, very hot summers in the southern hemisphere, cooler in the northern hemisphere summers will be very wet and winters dryer and colder…. more information later.

N: I give thanks.

Infinity

A: Our message for today is that of infinity. The infinite within all who exist on earth. Do you understand?

N: Clarification please.

A: Infinity is the God within in simplicity, one must recognise this in order for the light to shine, as people lose this connection to their infinity and the soul wanders in different directions, seeking and searching, lessons are learned in coming to the Godly self (the God within self) as in all people this must be recognised now to be in the light at all times, to assist in this Godly mission souls will be drawn to you, only light, others will shy away. Do not tire the self out just be, we are pleased at your work progress. Please keep on your path as it is very important to keep the connection with you without interference on a commercial level, write articles to speak on radio. This is building up to something better in communications, this is our message for today.

N: I give thanks.

Religion

A: Religion is structured and causing a lot of problems in the world. There is much stress in the Muslim world in Israel, with Jews and Muslims in Ireland with Catholic and Protestants alike. In Afghanistan with the strict regime. This we stress is not God's way.

Poem Titled
'Religion'

Religions are about power, each and every hour.

Love is the key for all mankind to see.

All religions will come together with the touch of an angel's feather.

Some folk are as tough as leather.

My advice to all is to stick together

Whether Muslim, Christian, Baha or Jews alike.

In this Aquarian age

Power can take a hike

Only love will win

That my child is no sin

As we approach two thousand and ten

The Atlantian essence

Will win.

Nollaig (Atlantis)

A: Atlantians were and are the purest ever to exist in thinking, lost in floods, the world needs to listen to our experiences. We lost all in the end through technology, science and experimentation, it is going to happen here now on the earthly plane if people do not stop and take note. As always, my child, tune in with us when on travels in the world we will always advise you my child. We were pure and bright and loving, to all, living the Godly way lost today, turn back to God now is the message of today otherwise many disasters will wipe out good and bad re: the balance.

N: Clarify please why good, I do not understand.

A: The good as above so below my child do not want all bad, souls here balance; balance sending out light to the world is needed now. Nollaig we wish to warn you of the dangers in the world and the up and coming youth in Ireland it is not the best now, charged with drugs and ammunition and thinking in a negative way, it is affecting the planet.

A: The time is correct now to warn humanity of our being in the spirit world. We want to warn of the many things that will affect the planet as we are enlightened and understand the changes.

N: What will happen please?

A: The planet is going to retaliate and have its say and it will happen soon.

N: When please?

A: Next two years 2007-2008 approx. around this time as the time is near to help planet.

Information for the crystal cross meditation for this time. The crystal cross is sacred in our name and is for this time in relation to the crystalline field in the body awakening now this is very important for those who are ready, but they must be ready.

The Crystalline Energy Field in the Body

A: Each person has this crystalline field around the physical, understand?

N: Yes.

A: Each person is evolving, understand?

N: Yes. Has it something to do with religion?

A: Religion and evolution is a contradiction in a way. Evolution is in the very being in the divinity of the whole person in relation to God, now this we want to make clear… Religion is made in a powerful confused way. Religion is very volatile in an open sense and being abused through fear e.g. fear of God. When the person comes into truth, divinity (that is recognising the God within), things become clear. Religion is ok, do not misunderstand but it teaches from without in a way there is no fear when God recognised that the soul repents, it does not need regimes, dictators… preaching from a high the church for example, this is not necessary all people have the power to come close to God. When truth in all matters is established this is what we are teaching and very important is the crystal body.

N: Is it in connection with evolution and how please?

A: The crystal body is more subtle than the physical… God aspiring and a lighter frequency on a different vibration, understand?

N: Yes.

A: So the energy needs purification and each person must be in truth to purify the light body. Activating this is very important in some people have no awareness of these higher frequency bodies. All have it within them. You have a bright energy frequency Nollaig through evolution, over a time all have to aspire to this. Complex but true, that will do my child.

Politics

A: Politics is not as it seems in England. Sold out to USA.

N: How please?

A: Trade and not democratic in a sense, greed and it is going against Europe, it will lead to much trouble in future times. Politicians are not in keeping with the transformation plan as many are in the ego state, need to send light to all politicians as follows: to Africa, Magabi, Russia, Pluton, to Bush in USA, to the European Parliament, in particular to the male dominance in this regime too much ego related power struggling men, more feminine energy in this EU state is necessary, not bad just out of balance. To the Pope, strength in his work a good man, to Northern Ireland Paisley and Gerry Adams peace is dawning and to the Scottish Parliament, to Israel and Egypt, the new president. To Iraq help is much needed in transformation of this country. In the whole plan what we are looking at from here is the globe. The deprived need help. What is required is a more balanced state for all to live in harmony, and above all in divinity. Is that clear?

N: Yes but please clarify things like leadership.

Leadership

A: Very well, leadership in the new world will be more balanced masculine with feminine energy, God/Goddess, priest/priestess and so on. At the moment all is male dominance and wanting in a greed way, that is not God's way. It is all about power, Europe is all about power. Europe is dictating the law to all its countries, this is not correct by buying countries with cash and then taking over in a way as we have said power is in the individual, power is in all and in recognising this evolution can grow in many ways. Dictatorship is over, it is stifling and interferes with the free will and free choice of the individual. Is that clear?

N: I give thanks.

Lecturing in the name of Atlantis

A: Our message for today is one of lecturing in our name. We want the world to know of the danger it is facing in the coming years, of the things that are happening and about to happen, to stall if possible through the circles of light in order to help the planet. Afghanistan is bad now, USA, and North Korea with its nuclear weapons is a threat to the west especially USA. In time to come things will get bad before getting better. So we want this message given out to all please. In our name the Atlantian essence, in time you will hold the council to the Atlantian lectures in Europe firstly then further afield. Do you understand this great mission?

N: Yes, I give thanks.

Trouble in England

N: What type of trouble please?

A: That of strikes within the EEC, that of money problems with sterling and dollar. People are not listening to their inner truths, false and false prophecy.

N: How please?

A: By listening to incorrect leaders being led in a false economic way. Do you understand my child?

N: Yes I do, much gratitude for information received.

A: We want you to communicate our message to the world soon.

N: What will I start with please?

A: The planet is in danger as we have said, the planet is in danger of attack by those that want power and to control, no freedom in this type of thinking of this powerful religious, spiritual dogmatic falsehood, not spiritual as they seem bad, evil and the world needs more focus on love. Now you will tell the world of the things that are about to happen.

N: What is about to happen please?

A: England is in danger still the police are not listening or acting fast enough in catching these evils ones. If they are not caught the people will suffer. An attack on democracy that is how it is, England must take note and be warned that soon Al Qaeda will not win but will attack. If these evil ones are not caught in England from Pakistan and other areas the attack could hit the north west power station for nuclear attack in England. The nature of this attack is England and USA only is Europe ok yet. Send light to the situation please to catch these planners, need to be stopped on their tracks before much devastation is caused on an international level.

N: (Light was sent out from the circles of light, transformation and truth. A number of Al Qaeda were caught in England with connections in Italy and other areas.)

A: Now to other matters in relation to your friend Elizabeth, not well, not good at all later we will inform, free will and as always free choice.

N: (My friend from Austria who had received much information passed to spirit in September 2004. It is sad her vibration lowered in a commercial world and influence).

A: Please send the light urgently to the English situation, divert, defuse and catch the evil ones, not a good situation at all. Pakistan and all types of Muslim extreme groups involved, no dictators, not the way, it is time now to get these people out of the areas.

N: Where are they please?

A: North West England and South London

N: (Have been caught since going to print, the light has won. We must shine the light to dark areas and it will win).

A: We are here to lead, guide and educate in spiritual maturity with our earthly accumulation of wisdom and knowledge combined with the spiritual experience of evolution in the light.

Atlantis was the best place on earth, most highly evolved beings, we have the knowledge for the planet to be saved, always learn from mistakes, we do not want the same thing to happen to planet earth. The planet is retaliating now to the abuse by many, it simply cannot take any more, in time it will change and many will die and this is all part of the transformation. People are not listening and will need to adjust and to come in line with the great plan:

N: Why will they die please?

A: By die we mean in light, soul not ready or not at level of vibration for this great change on the planet and shock treatment with health etc will hold on a set vibration at a lower frequency. Do you understand?

N: Yes.

A: In time animals will be free from abuse…

N: This is great news.

People

A: Nollaig today we would like to talk of people.

N: What type of people?

A: All people on planet earth are evolving at a terrific rate now, the time is near for this great transformation on the planet. Some will suffer, some will evolve, some will be held back for this time. Understand?

N: Yes and no, please clarify.

A: What we are saying is that all are the same, but at different stages of evolution hence they will evolve at different times, in different ways, re: the lesson state. Understand?

N: Yes.

A: Much help is at hand now for those souls who are ready but once again they must be ready, you are ready, you are gifted in channelling with our help as you always acknowledge, this is good, you will help shift many souls now. In the next two years be ready take care of the physical and aspects of the self, be centred, be single minded, be alert, in body be in the now, this is very important Nollaig. The now is where power is, you know this knowledge, use it, tune in every day now. Now to other matters. War. In Jerusalem is going to get very serious soon.

War

A: USA is causing many problems here, this will change on a global level soon: Afghanistan will suffer.

N: At the hands of who please?

A: The world, Europe and USA combined. Italy will be next hit. Then UK.

N: Is this true?

A: Yes.

N: Anything else?

A: On war no. Europe will dictate to its people, this is not a good thing, male dominated and too much ego power related, property will drop in UK soon Ireland will suffer too re: inflation.

N: Who are you please?

A: We are your higher knowledgeable beings the Mayan and Atlantian of the Christ the essence energy always at hand to help.

Atlantis use of Solar and Wind Energy

A: Now we will start our conversation today on a high vibration that you can reach. Our conversation contains information on Atlantis.

Atlantis is and was one of the best in the earth's history. We knew much. We experimented in science as today, but we were far more advanced than the science today. We were working in all natural resources, solar energy, water energy and the wind. These were the natural resources available to us at the time as today things on the planet are always at hand and natural. It is the interference that causes the problems like today. Nuclear is not the correct way to go, please emphasise this. We would like you to write soon and get this information out. This is the main request today. You will feel enlightened and not tired when you express our wishes and the way ahead. You will write much in our name in the near future.

You will in time learn that in letting all past issues go, they will return threefold. That is the nature of the law when you tune into it. Ask for the correct things to suit the purpose in life and lifestyle. You shall receive. Now to other matters relating to the planet. The planet is retaliating very much at the moment and it will cause much panic in people soon. As we have mentioned in the next three years approximately.

N: With whom do I speak?

A: I am 'St. Germain' your highly evolved master working on the transformation plan in favour of mankind and the planet.

N: As always much gratitude for information given.

A: We warn once again of the world's plight in relation to terror. It will get bad in the future, understand?

N: Clarification please.

A: Well we want the world to take note and not to be taken in by governments. This needs to be highlighted to the public now. Is that clear?

N: Yes.

Climate

A: The climate is retaliating now to the people and the future will be exciting with events unfolding on a global level. The temperatures will fall swiftly this winter. That is how it will be, the people will stop and take note of the information as the imbalance is being felt now and it will in time be very significant my child, that is it as we have said before, seas will rise causing flooding, waters in England and France combined with violence will be very bad.

Now in time the world will slow a little, it is essential as it is moving too fast. Godly energy, this energy we speak of the Christ essence is on a subtle level. The world is mental and fast moving and not in co-operation. Technology as we have said, many times sunk us, we have the knowledge and we want peace. It is very important to go forward in the transformation plan, emphasise this. The time is correct for change from negativity to a Godly way of life. It is out of control. We beg the people to listen or it will be too late. Please get this message out soon.

Great to be alive
More information from Atlantis

East – West Relations 2005 – 2009

A: Things will take time to reach a peak the next few years will see many changes.

N: Is it war?

A: A possibility as it is needed on earth now, as darkness is strong in influence and things will and must happen to quieten all, within two or three years perhaps. USA and N. Korea is a danger to each other now. It could trigger off a disturbance in East-West relations, all a possibility in time. For now keep writing and processing print, soon all that is given to date. Lots more information to follow.

Warning

A: We wish to warn once again of the world's plight in relation to terror. It will get bad in the future. Jordan, Syria, Egypt and neighbouring countries. This will be highlighted in the near future, Israel in the firing line. The Muslim states are getting together against the West. A very dangerous situation for mankind and Turkey is involved.

N: What will happen please?

A: It is too soon to say, planning is underway as we communicate. It can be stalled though circles of light.

N: With whom do I speak?

A: St Germain in light.

Copy of Registered Letter
To No 10 Downing Street
London WC1, ENGLAND
Nollaig McKeogh

Floantilles C.P. Int
San Miguel De Salinas
03193 San Miguel Road
Alicante
Spain, Europe

Tel: 0034 639 279 707

18/11/2005

Dear Mr. Blair

Please note the following information has been channelled though myself. The source is the Atlantian Ancient Civilisation, lost in earthquakes and tidal waves and floods. Warning the world of future dangers that lie ahead, if mankind do not stop the slaughter and revert back to peace, you or whoever is reading this information now please stop.

Do we want peace or war? To date many prophecies have taken place as a result of information received, foot and mouth disease, America in trouble as a result of Karmic debt to the world, trouble in Kashmir, do I need to go on? This is accurate information but nobody is listening.

It is my second letter to Downing Street. So please, please listen to what is coming though.

Please put me in touch with United Nations, EEC. As you are well in here or Scotland Yard. If you would like to receive this very important information received on October 26th 2005 as follows:

Today we wish to warn of things in the near future.
Things will happen in Egypt in the nature of governments and corruption
with governments and tourists soon, in a religious type of rebellion to Islam, fundamentalists, Israel is again in danger. This is not a good mix and Muslim terrorists will rise again approx Christmas panic will start.

Now to Jordan: In trouble and in time Jordan will be governed by other Arab States. This will cause much conflict in the future Arab world, and of course with oil as Jordan was the best most evolved state, in the Arab world. Send light to Jordan. The planet needs urgent help or it will be shocked into war, as it is titled in a negative way and is triggering off global disasters. It cannot take much more of this.

We wish to warn the governments that the planning is underway with tourism in Egypt and other related areas, Jordan as we gave yesterday will be affected most of all, Turkey is involved in this evil corrupt way and must be stalled by the United Nations. Turkey is a danger to the Western World by leadership of the extreme groups. They do not want tourism and will hit hard.

Turkey must not get further power in Europe, this is very important.

Info Received Nov 11th 2005

The Atlantian civilisation want to help the world. The planet must please listen. This is a request now, the world is in danger to East by America, United Nations needs to do something.

Lots more information received, could you please state Mr Blair, if you would like my help in passing on this very important, powerful information to EEC, to America, to United Nations, to people like Bob Geldof and his plight or whoever you suggest in your high position on a global level. Please let me have e-mails and telephone numbers.

Please reply ASAP.

Will register this letter with information and will hold incoming information until I hear from you. I will take this opportunity to wish you well at Downing Street. Please hang on in there as the world needs you and the opposition may even cause more problems re: cracking down on terrorism.

Yours sincerely in love, light and truth.

_____

Nollaig McKeogh

Colour Therapist Channel for Atlantis Global Healing

P.S. Also received information re: London underground was in danger last year telling me not to travel to London, Birmingham and Liverpool target areas. Re: planet – London and Jersey will eventually be under water. Thames barrier vulnerable. Lots more. Adiós.

Pope John Paul

A: Changes will happen when the new pope is elected that of the outlook in the world. The world needs a good Pope in love, it will be controversial for a time.

N: How please?

A: Well political in a way all craving for power in the church. The people have shown the popularity of Pope John Paul and should be listened to. People need to speak out now. No dictatorship, all leaders think they are more important than subjects. This, we stress, is not the way forward, teach from this angle Nollaig.

Say that in time Christianity will win, it is going through a transformation. John Paul can do much from here through his followers, his shepherds, and they will make history. We are in this vibration. Stick with his way, his teachings, his humility and his wit, his gentle but firm way. We want this please.

Terrorism is not over at all, only stalled for now. The royals will eventually go, not in keeping with Europe and expensive. People have enough of nonsense and looking deeper now, not interested in frills, for now things will carry on in a silly fashion. Those changes will occur by means of votes, climate change, terror etc.

Justice is very important to people. God's way on earth. Raising the earthly vibration send out the light from Lourdes on your travels and from Mount St. Michael. it is St. Michael's request. This is a special trip, you are doing great work all round as an earthly being, well done.

Now we, the Atlantian Civilisation once again wish to warn all humanity that we are at hand to help in the transformation plan. Never before in the history of mankind has so much help been available. It is all to do with evolution and that is great.

People are evolving very fast now. With technology well advanced in the brain etc. We can communicate when truth is acknowledged, we worked very hard and mined crystals and much more. In time we will communicate more on us, our dress, our style, our way of life when ready. You must communicate what has been received to date please.

Now we want to talk of shepherds of Christ like the Pope John Paul. Pray for this please, pray for more lay shepherds, preachers in a humble way when the new Pope comes. Please pray to the Pope, a saint here ascended now like St. Germain:

N: With whom do I speak?

A: I am 'Jacob' in connection with ascension.

N: Much gratitude for information received.

Inflation 2005-2009

A: Today we wish to warn of the things to come on a monetary level. The dollar is dropping and it will affect sterling, this in turn will affect the euro and inflation will rocket, to an all time high. Do you understand this?

N: Yes, but what will happen to the euro please?

A: Well my child the things to come include the effects on family life, houses and cars. Dominance from governments in Ireland and blame to Europe. All are to blame in this greedy crazy world. Leaders are wrong in many ways. They are not listening to their people who gave them the power to destroy. People will suffer as a result of this soon. The coming three to four years it will start to affect people. Oil will rocket as a result of the American dollar and leadership is playing games with Europe. It is not fair to mankind. Things will be bad in Ireland, cold, very cold and expensive.

N: Can you tell me something about your civilisation and your life on earth please?

A: It was powerful in the end, and power is what sunk us. Purity is necessary to evolve in this particular time. The ascension process is not about power. We make the mistake. Power in materialism is not the way now. Power in balance is what is needed from where we are, it's plain to be seen. Rise above earthly powers in materialism, do not become part of it, be smart, be educated and be humble. Be charming but do not get caught up in this earthly struggle in a competitive world. It is not the way.

A: Power is in purity. Teach from this prospective, do not look up to, or down upon anybody. This is ego related and not of our pure essence. Now to end this conversation farewell on the note of light and love and peace in the self. Write this information in the name of Atlantis, I remain St. Germaine of the Christ Essence.

N: I will carry out your request with much gratitude for these words of wisdom.

Turkey in East/West Relations

A: Now we greet you with love and warning in the things to come on a commercial level in Europe. It is only starting now, job loss etc. Setting up the eastern part of EEC is a game as such as it will take back much from the west. Now it is payback time in this silly game but not all bad. The oil is affected by climate and war. This is the control side of things and it will get much worse. The time is correct now to go forward with messages received in our name.

Now to America: This is a type of karma coming back to the people and Bush is not good for this country. New leadership is necessary and it will come to the USA. It is essential for the changes affecting the world now and in the coming years. Terrorism is quiet for now but wait and see, these evil ones are working on other projects. It will be a disaster for Italy if they go ahead. The network needs to be stopped urgently. As it is gaining much power within Europe and the Muslim faith. We want to warn the world of this please. Europe is giving too much power to Turkey, this we stress is not advisable. Europe must hold these people in a different category to western countries. Turks' attitude to the west is one of power and trouble. With Turkey trying to control the EU, this is not a good situation all round but it is part of the change and the free will and Europe. Not good at all we advise to hold western countries separate. They will not integrate quietly.

The sterling in UK will drop to an all time low, this will quieten many. That is how it is. This is the information for today, we advise you to get ready to write our manuscript, meditate and heal the self. We await your raised energy.

N: I give thanks for this information: Who are you please?

A: Jacob 'the philosopher' on the ascension process my child.

The Figure 8 and the Eight Meditation, Healing from Atlantis

A: All healing comes from the heart centre and this is so. However one needs to open up to the love in all things. This is the most important thing in any healing, opening and closing of the heart centre in order for the frequency to come in from above. Work on the heart centre everyday through the eight meditation as this speeds up the vibration on the earthly plane. This is very important, colours etc as in colour, colour breathing will lift the vibration. Must reach this stage to work and to communicate with us. Please tell those that come to the meditation class. This is very important. We want to see more people meditating on the 8th meditation:

People like it, but they simply are not practising. Promote in a different way as follows figure 8, we will advise on eight once again: by this figure one is connected to the physical and spiritual aspects of the whole being, which is important to exist. The body is just matter, without the soul. The soul is the most important aspect. The body is secondary as it houses the soul. This is the lesson for today and everyday please adhere to it. The eight meditation works on taking issues from matter and transforming them into light cleansing and healing while at the same time centring in the heart. Using colours green and pink become revitalised, re-energised, re-awakened and re-invented in this meditation: That will do, get this out in meditation workshop when the time is correct. (See 8th meditation also recorded on CD - page 159).

Now to other matters in relation to judgement, you must not judge anybody, anytime in healing, in life and in general. It lowers vibration and it is not in our vibration. Raise above all communications in the ego, understand? This is your pure path.

N: Yes, in gratitude.

Fortunes

A: Very well we will like to discuss that of fortunes. Fortunes are rare on the earthly plane, in our time we had fortunes in wealth, in the correct way in balance my child. We are striving for balance here with humanity for fortunes. Fortunes are more important than Godly wealth but people do not see that later fortunes are of no value here in light. This causes trouble for many souls on earth.

N: Do you mean on earth or in light later?

A: Later, causing trouble in a sense by means of blocking spiritual growth and holding the soul on a lower level. All must aspire in hierarchy, nearer to God. That is how it is here. It is pure, it is beautiful, it is free for those who have dealt with their karma and lessons on earth my child. That is the end of our lecture on healing for today. Read, digest soon please.

Errors in Humanity and Karma

A: Today we wish to speak about the errors in humanity. Humanity will have to evolve now. It is a great time to evolve in the physical body, this is so. Humanity will know own truths eventually but for now mankind keep on making karma: This is the cause of much trouble in the world, understand?

N: Clarity on karma please.

A: By that we mean that all in the physical body will need to adjust frequency and raise the vibration in order to come nearer to God. This opportunity is available now for those that are listening and indeed those that are ready to evolve at this time on earth. This is the very important lesson today.

Poetry

A: My child, now we wish to tell you of our experiences in poetry. At this point we would like you to set up a creative writing or inspirational writers' circles with poetry in the near future. We love poetry, we wrote much in our time on the continent of Atlantis. That of a romantic nature and humour, it is very important in this area.

Poem Titled
'The Poetry Ball'

The Atlantians are sunk, this is so
But evolution did not go astray
As while in our earthly frames we sang,
We danced, we evolved and did much work on the planet
We are, and were close to God and that accounts for all
When our continent had a great fall.
So my child in poetry
You will have a great ball.
This is the lord's call
Deliver much through the verses
This is what you are versed in.

A: That will do, tune in tomorrow

N: I will tune in tomorrow, much gratitude for the poem.

Oil

A: Today we wish to warn you of the many things that will happen in the near future. Oil will stop the economy in its tracks by means of stalling things.

N: Is this true?

A: Well yes, the economy depends on oil and oil is the bait. The bait is now in trouble and it will stall machinery, planes and more, household heat and electricity etc, it will be bad for a time and it is necessary. Now to other matters relating to the planet, war in Afghanistan will trigger off things in India, North Korea with USA as a result of frustration with the people, will retaliate against the USA soon, watch and see this will happen and it will be bad. The crisis in these poor countries is a result of corruption my child, greed and corruption behind the scenes. The people are suffering, this is not correct at all in God's eyes. It is a deadly sin and must stop in the government, in ruling and in lack of love. It is not correct and America will suffer soon again, as Afghanistan blame them for taking power from the east. It is true my child and it will get bad, forming a world collapsed economy that of oil, and that of governments, that is all.

Atlantis Essence and Matrix of Body and Planet

A: The essence of Atlantis is pure, as we have mentioned many times. It is pure in thought, in truth and in keeping with God's plan. Is that clear?

N: Clarification of essence in purity with God please?

A: The essence is at its highest now at this time of evolution, lessons learned on the earthly time and the progress here since repentance, the realisation of wrongdoings in the end and so on, is that clearer?

N: Yes, what wrongdoings please?

A: Later, but for now we would like to talk only on the purity of Atlantis.

Purity of Atlantis

A: The purity of Atlantis was never achieved again at the same level but through the 'Golden Age' coming about now the essence can be reached at this time. If the people will stop, turn back to God, repent and listen. This is the request for today's people and they need to know this as they are searching in vain and they will not find what they search for outside of themselves. The help is at hand to find the essence within, this is the divinity in all. It is not outside but within the whole matrix of the body. Is that clear?

N: Define matrix please?

A: By matrix we simply mean the whole make-up of the energy field in purity. In the light body, the matrix vibrates on a higher frequency possible to be achieved with our help at this particular time on earth. The matrix is always there in energy field, but the souls cannot reach this higher frequency through negative thinking. Is that clear?

N: Yes.

A: The eight meditation is about raising the physical body to this matrix body.

Matrix of the Planet

A: We will now move on to the other matters relating to the planet and the matrix of the planet. This is damaged. The higher frequency is damaged and the protective layers penetrating through are too strong for the energy field of the body as it needs protection.

N: Is it from cancer?

A: Yes in a way, as the rays omitted can be harmful and this is so, but in the purity of the essence of Atlantis, the body can rise to a higher frequency and raise above matter. Do you understand?

N: I thought rising above matter was in dying, could you please clarify?

A: In rising above matter is about dying and this is what all people will do in the end, but while in the physical body it is still possible to evolve at a greater speed now we evolve in the light at a very fast frequency compared to earth, but raising a little above the earthly body, it is possible to achieve more this time. That will do, complicated a little. For you to understand. Will be clearer later my child. When the work to date is published.

N: Hopefully by 2008-09, I give thanks.

Information as follows on topic 2006 – 2009 and Beyond.
(Received Christmas December 2005)

A: Our topic for today is on humanity in relation to governments. The information that we will deliver through you is very important in relation to the evolution of mankind. Do you understand?

N: Yes.

Humanity and Governments 2006-2009 and Beyond

A: Very well then we would like to mention that of

(a) humanity in relation to governments in 2006-2009 and beyond. Humanity will stand up more for the planet and will not just take what is given, but only some who are ready. This is the correct thing in taking back the power for those at that evolutionary stage. Not all will feel this power in energy, as they are at different stages in the soul's lesson state.

(b) Then comes the retaliation from churches when one speaks out. The church may retaliate as it is trying very hard now to control, but it has lost out in the mishandling of the people in the past. The people in this millennium hold the key to self evolvement or to helping the self raise nearer to the almighty who is ever forgiving, at this special time on earth when repentance is acknowledged. Please emphasise this in writings. You are our scribe in delivering these sacred words from a high. St. Germain.

N: Thank you for this information.

Climate – Changes needed in relation to planet, terrorism knowledge.

Received on Christmas Day

We would like to talk on various topics today as follows:

- **Climate and the changes in store for humanity in the next couple of years approximately 2006-2008 and beyond.**
- **People and the changes needed in relation to the planet.**
- **How the world is in danger re: terrorism.**
- **Your work in relation to getting out the message.**
- **Knowledge**

Now we wish to greet you in light, as we are in light and we wish to thank you once again for the great work being done and patience is needed now. We are as always working on the correct souls and energy for this mission, it is very urgent. It, we stress cannot be rushed in any way. The best advice today is to relax into the whole experience of Atlantis. It is a very important mission, but do not take it seriously, in a way, you need joy in your earthly life. Do you understand?

N: Not exactly, please clarify.

A: Well, dance, get out and have fun: Humour is important, but discipline in our work. Do not mix work in a social way. Listen, step back and allow the fun all round. Recognising the stages of evolution. Just sowing seeds but not in a dictatorial way, this is very important. Do you understand?

N: Yes.

A: We will now move on to next topic, the planet. In the next couple of years and beyond snow melt is going to cause much problems this winter in the west of England, the northern hemisphere, in Spain, in Canada and other areas Austria, Mt. Blanc and Eastern France, Scotland and north east of England. When the seas rise the rivers will swell and the flooding will be great in spring March/April (approx.). This is a time when many will panic and the houses will be under water in some areas, the people will start searching for something to try to understand. The climate, the changes and the people will react to the leadership and governments. A type of war of words and the green peace against the governments and their policies in nuclear gas.

N: Is nuclear gas a good thing or bad, is it bad for the world please?

A: Well as we see it from here bad and it is not the way forward, only natural systems are needed for the world that is all on the climate for now, we want to warn that the people need to get in line now.

N: How please, any tips?

A: Yes – they need to stop the extravagance in waste, too much waste in energy, in fuel, in gas, in all. Energy needs to be natural and it needs to be reserved. Energy needs to be in keeping with the planet. They will have to start the natural plans as soon as possible, this is what is necessary. Natural windmills, there is enough of natural resources around eg sea water which creates energy, wind energy. It is the natural way to go. Nuclear, we stress, is a dangerous business to venture into. It will take much debating in England with trouble from the green party.

N: Why is it dangerous please?

A: Emissions into the atmosphere and the interference with the energy field of the human being. This is not natural in keeping with the atmosphere and in tense energy. It is advanced, it is expensive but it is not what the planet needs. Wave energy, windmills and solar energy is what we advise. Please stress this. We would like this in writing by means of an article on the planet soon.

N: Yes, I will carry out this wish.

A: Now to people. People will adapt to the needs of the planet soon, so it is the correct time to write articles. They will see things in a different light, we would like you to pass this information on to mankind.

Next to the power of people.

People need to take back their own power soon as they have the power (after the planet). We would like to point out that the planet has the power to look after mankind, but there needs to be a balance struck soon as the people are taking only and polluting more and more and the gasses are affecting oxygen levels in turn affect winds and so on. Do you understand this information?

N: I need a little more clarification please.

A: The trees emit oxygen this is so, the oxygen clears the air, but the people do not understand this. They cut down the trees and that is the way in the world. This is wrong. Elephants are eating the trees. Why? They are not being looked after by the people. This is another issue for later.

Knowledge

A: We would like to talk a little today on knowledge. You have knowledge through us. This is a very privileged position to be in on earth at this particular time. The knowledge that we speak of is our wisdom in relaying information in prophecies etc. All the prophecies have come to pass, well most of them in any case and the planet needs more people like you to communicate. This is extremely important now as the planet is tilted in a negative direction. The next couple of years and beyond will bring many changes. The people are beginning to get in touch with themselves, they are searching amongst the pain in life and know that materialism is not the way. Education and humility is the way. Christ was humble, God is humble and power is in humility Nollaig, do not lose this.

N: Thank you for the lesson and knowledge. I remain your humble channel in gratitude as always.

Human Trafficking

A: It is on the increase and human trafficking is out of control now. This we stress is all through greed (greed in the people). It is getting worse. Drugs are the same as greed and materialism is the scourge of mankind. The peace is lacking and the peace needs to be restored in order for the soul to evolve. That will do for now my child. You will learn fast and we will inform. For the soul to evolve you must publish our writings soon. Is that clear?

N: Yes, I will as I value this wisdom.

A: Very well my child, we will bid you adieu for today. Tune in soon please.

N: I will tune in tomorrow if and when possible. I give thanks as always in love, light and truth.

Mankind is in Need of Long Term Fix

The Changing Face of our Planet

A: Warning the world at this time of a shift in a negative direction balance must be achieved now in order to go forward. It is imminent and the biggest problem facing the world this decade and beyond. It is a crucial time in the history of mankind. The shift in the living earth is promoting a sense of urgency. It is spiralling out of control and people in power are not listening.

Would you like to help by taking back your personal power coupled with giving positive energy to our planet, to help re-balance in a positive way? We are all at fault in this; if the answer is yes then carry on reading.

Well the Atlantian civilisation know much re: the changes coming to our planet. This is not just a mythical civilisation who disappeared some place out there in the Atlantic ocean (well it may be partly true) but the truth is that these highly evolved souls, sunk themselves through greed and getting above themselves experimenting with technology etc. They from a higher dimension wish to warn mankind now that we are in danger of the same thing millions of years later, listen to their words of wisdom please, this is their plight. The continent of Atlantis was pure; the civilisation of that era only used natural resources and worked hard on the land. The ancient civilisation known as the Atlantians lost all through progress as they got above themselves, tilted the balance and caused a catastrophe in the sea.

They are warning today of the many changes taking place and explain how we can help by raising the vibration on earth simply by sending light to dark areas. The light will triumph in the end. Please listen to the highly evolved civilisation who warn that we are in danger of repeating history. Please get together with like-minded people in prayer, affirmation in healing circles in various countries, this will help to bring in light and allow the Golden Age to dawn once again.

The northern hemisphere is changing in Europe. It is the start of a cycle, a pattern, the cycle is going to continue for a number of years, 5 years approx. Starting now 2006-2011 and continuing, getting worse as we speak. Snow from the arctic affects seas, water rising in return affecting the rivers, then the banks burst and so on. Our civilisation achieved more than today's peoples still under water in the Atlantic Ocean. it will be highlighted one day. Please listen to our advice.

N: Yes, I will pass this information on with much gratitude on planetary information and on all information received to date.

Ascended Masters and Violet Flame

A: Today we wish to inform in the name of Atlantis teachings according to the ascended ones 'St. Germain', Jesus and the highly evolved ones in God's name and in the Christ essence. Is that clear my child?

N: Yes and no, is Jesus and St. Germain on the very same vibration now.

A: Yes, and they are bringing about change. St. Germain in this age and Jesus two thousand years ago and the Golden Age is the age for this highly evolved time. During Jesus' time on earth people were not at the stage possible for this age to reign but now it is possible for this age to reign with the help of the violet flame and me, Germain.

N: How please?

A: Well in time many souls will come on to their own awakening, this is the automatic process on this ascension path, but now through the violet flame. The time for cleansing hastens.

N: Yes, but was the violet flame available during Jesus' time?

A: No, not released, understand?

N: Yes.

A: Now we will proceed my fair one. During this time of Aquarius and the urgency of the planet, the help is at hand to bring those souls forward in love through Reiki, love, repentance, which we have referred to many times, the hasty evolution is possible now to bring in this golden age, people must stop and turn back to God in love, in truth, in forgiveness and all will be well. But they are not listening. Materialism is winning now and the urgency is at hand. We want the people to listen to our messages please as follows. In time to come the world will change, the suffering will ease and the new age will dawn. Work to do now for those that will participate, the rewards will be high on the next level. Please tell the people that material wealth is of no use here once again: nobody to impress in light all the same in God's eyes and we are helping people now to be ready for this level as all will eventually come here and all must know that through their earthly doings they will ascend. The time is correct now to balance the karma in all souls, this is the urgency to do this, but one must be in truth. This is the most important part of the ascension journey, be in own truth and then radiate out the truth in all things in a very commercial world. This is difficult we appreciate but rising above in a charming charismatic way will and can help to see the souls wants and needs and allow the body to merge rather than seeing the body's needs and allowing the soul to merge occasionally. This is our message to you today Nollaig.

N: I give thanks.

Hamas

A: We want to inform of the many things in the Middle East now, things will get very, very serious, through Hamas, a type of dictatorship in a subtle way not as it seems the organisation.

N: How please?

A: Well they want to dictate to Israel and Europe have the power through United Nations. This power is a threat to them and they will try to diminish or break it.

N: Is that true?

A: Yes, corruption on Hamas is about to be viewed by the western world.

N: How Please?

A: They will try to dictate without diplomacy and will not win, this is the very important message, send light here and tell the circles that this is a dangerous situation for Europe as follows. Hamas does not like the highlight and interference from outside world and Europe are wonderful at communication in these movements. Egypt is the same does not want this, they want power and money and ammunition but does not want to bend in any at all to gain this, let them off. Now light and more circles are needed in the world. The war will start within themselves and they do not want westerners involved, they will kill anybody who does not go with them. The peace process here will not exist for a while and the negativity will have to come out eventually, a new dawning will evolve but Bush and Hamas will not be part of it. They will be caught and organisations squashed eventually like Saddam Hussein. Dictators will never let go until they die and they all have to go. Europe needs to be very careful now once again with Turkey, it is involved with these dictatorships and not all good for Europe.

Global Warming 2006 – 2016

A: Well Nollaig we wish to advise this time of the effects of global warming. When things heat up on the planet it causes an imbalance like a turbulence, heat and air. This is so the extreme temperatures that will be felt in the future are starting now and will continue over the next ten years and beyond. This decade is going to see many changes on the surface of the earth. For example higher sea levels, floods and erosion. The climate will cause problems in people and winters will be colder in northern hemisphere and hotter in southern hemisphere and people are too caught up in their own wants and needs to stop and take note of what is evolving on earth. In time the people will begin to see changes and will question their existence and direction etc. Do you understand?

N: Yes.

A: This is where you/we will come in with the wisdom of Atlantis. The Atlantians were kind to the atmosphere and nurtured the very earth that gave us all. We respected the spirit in all animal, mineral and were at one with all. Mankind is losing this now on a level that is contactable. People know this, the awakening and awareness needs a little push and encouragement and in time all will come to the realisation that God is all. Love is all and that we are all part of the whole whatever the religion, political views and so on. This is our message for you today Nollaig.

N: I give thanks.

Peace, Love and Light

A: We would like to start our conversation with peace and love and light as a civilisation that understood the needs for this. We want to share with you the need on many levels, the need in humanity for peace. All are striving for peace in the soul and the peace we talk about is one of the Godly source that all are aspiring to and that is the ultimate on this level in light, understand?

N: Yes and no, clarification please.

Evolution

A: Well the soul seeks peace, this is so. Peace is what brings happiness always. When the soul leaves the body peace is ultimate but can be achieved now through evolution, through us and this is very important, people do not understand evolution.

Evolution is why we/you are here on this level and on the next level. It is what we aspire to nearer to God. Please do not listen to those who will say they do not believe in this only fear based on evolution is what we are all about on the planet and on the next level closer to God, do you now understand?

N: Yes I do.

A: Then we will move swiftly. We are in light and we like to share with mankind all days important in the spirit world. You will in time become famous through us as we have insight above humanity about the world and where it is going. We want to share with humanity and we wish to ask questions of humanity. Why am I here? Where am I going? Can I take my material wealth with me? And what can I do to help God and the planet to evolve. This is not the whole picture as some would think or see but the broader picture is what we are interested in regarding to evolution Nollaig. That is all on this subject for now.

N: I give thanks.

Property and Rising House Rates

A: We wish to warn now of the coming things oil will be a problem in the autumn and rising house rates. A monetary problem ahead with the banks, the Euro and the sterling which will affect property. It is a good time to sell now. The time is correct to speak of us my child. Do not be afraid to speak out. It is perfectly alright to feel sad at people's attitudes. It is the stage that they are at. Do not let it stall your work. We want to warn of the things on the planet from now until the end of the year as follows:

Middle East will get out of hand and affect the west. Oil and currency will trigger off a world recession in a way, property and other essentials like food, trade, travel and so on: You must warn of this and that the people are living on borrowed money and not facing up to the real world. The world is in danger to the Middle East and oil is the bait here. We leave you in peace until our next connection.

N: Thank you for this valuable information.

Honesty

A: Our message for today is one of honesty and truth. Honesty in the self is number one, then truth is born out of honesty. Truth is in our pure energy. It is on the eight ray or vibration. The eight vibration as we have give on 8th meditation is a high vibration to reach the planet is struggling as it is shifting and the people are not shifting fast enough which causes an imbalance. It needs positive thought power and it needs power and light. Is that clear?

N: Yes, but how can people help if they are not ready for this vibration?

A: Well only those in awareness or evolutionary state can help. This is a crucial point, others will be left at a learning stage when things happen. They will get the chance again, but this time for those in our vibration can do much to help with this very rewarding work. We want you to announce this. We want more help in the world please. It is our request we need help with sending light to dark areas to governments, religions, countries and animals.
I remain Germain your guide in this great plan:

N: Thank you St. Germain.

Divinity

A: Well Nollaig our message is one of divinity. True divinity is being re-aligned, now this is the very important message today and it is awakening in the souls of those who have the knowledge to communicate it wisely and with our help in this great plan will work. You are doing wonderful work now and we appreciate the input in this work will be greatly rewarded for putting these great souls on paths and encouragement to you for this work. Not easy but worthwhile and you win in all areas of healing.

N: Much gratitude.

Atlantis connects
direct from heaven

Tough Times Ahead

A: As always we are at hand to help and we wish to warn of the coming events in the world. Times ahead will be tough in a climatic atmosphere. People need to adjust now and stop the commercial spending. It is out of proportion. Personal power needs to be taken back now. It is urgent. People also need to protect the immune system. Older people in particular will not have the capacity to adjust to the colder climate, it is coming too quickly.

This is all part of the transformation plan and it is to warn the hungry, greedy humans above themselves. We the Atlantians are for the planet and we are for the welfare of all. We want to help but people must listen. Please tell them once again for the saviour of mankind. We wish to transmit our information but people have to be ready. It will take time and patience is necessary. All is in order to go forward now with our blessings. I remain St. Germain.

N: As always, I give thanks for the information received.

Attitudes

A: 2007 is going to be a year of light and change in people's attitudes. We are in your best interest in this great work and we want to help in anyway possible. By means of healing, communicating and information prophecies and more, that of writing ancient and sacred writings in our name. people will seek contentment, inner peace and will begin to question the purpose in life and they will be more open to your/our work, understand?

N: Yes, but how please?

A: They will begin to appreciate advice more and will help in planetary work. Now is the time to speak out, to write and to inform. We are with you in help and guidance. People at this stage of evolution must look within and reconnect to the divine. They will not find divinity in materialism outside of the self. That is all for now my child. Tune in later.

N: Gratitude as always for this valuable wisdom of Atlantis.

Coming Events in Spain

A: Today we wish to inform of the coming events in Spain: The freedom in people is inhibited in a democratic society. This is not good enough as people have fear and this is not acceptable. The eastern Europeans are partly to blame, together with corrupt police, not doing their job. It is out of hand now and the people need to speak out.

Purity in the Atlantian Essence

A: It is time to re-introduce our 'Golden Atlantis' purity back into the evolutionary state of mankind. Do you understand this?

N: A little clarification re: re-introduction please?

A: By that we mean at this time on earth as earthly beings and lessons over time. It is correct to go forward with our advice, our warnings before it is too late to save the planet.

N: How long do we have please?

A: Well, it will be revealed soon.

N: How please?

A: In different ways to stop the violence and the starvation, the hardship, the dictatorship and the confusion in mankind. It is not the way only purity in our time being lost now to ego related greed in all ways and in all societies, losing the Godly divinity in the essence. We wish to warn of the dangers in losing the focus on divinity in all human beings. The soul must go forward from this plane. It must repent, and conform to universal laws. Otherwise it is lost, vulnerable and stuck. Please pass this message on.

N: Yes I will, with whom do I speak?

A: St. Germain of the transformation programme my child, thank you for your commitment.

St. Germain

A: Once again, we are your Atlantian forbearers of the earth, now in spirit and we are helping with planetary transformation under the guidance of 'St. Germain', do you understand?

N: Is St. Germain above you in spirit?

A: He is an ascended master and in control or in charge of the transformation light violet flame to earth at this very important time now in 2007.

N: Is Jesus and St. Germain equal in spirit?

A: Both are masters and both are near to God the almighty.

N: Where do you fit in please?

A: We are near to God and assisting with this plan on earth. You will know through St. Germain.

N: I am confused, did St. Germain live as an Atlantian, yes or no please?

A: Yes, this is so; we are all including St. Germain of Atlantian and the Christ essence. Jesus is a master in records.

N: Is it earthly records?

A: Yes, St. Germain is working for the salvation of mankind like Jesus while on earth two thousand years ago. Do you understand?

N: Please clarify.

A: St. Germain now, Jesus then, both are the same in God's work with mankind. Is that clear?

N: Yes I understand now and I give thanks for clarification.

The Holy Spirit

A: We wish to talk on the topic of the Holy Spirit today. The Holy Spirit is in all humankind but lost in negativity. The Holy Spirit needs to shine now in humanity, light is needed for the Holy Spirit to work through and this is very important. Acknowledgement of same is necessary now at this time on earth. Do you understand?

N: No, could you clarify a little please.

A: The Holy Spirit is the spirit within all humanity, some have lost this and are searching now. It must be connected at this time to help with the vibration on earth.

N: Is this the linking of spirit to matter as in the figure 8 and the eight meditation?

A: Yes it is, when this happens in truth, it will become automatic. Is that clear?

N: Yes.

A: Holy Spirit will help when in own truth, this is very important take this on board your mission.

Christian Faith in Ireland being lost within Europe

A: We wish to inform of the future events in Ireland. The Irish People are giving too much to the religious groups and they are in danger of democracy being affected.

N: Any tips for Ireland please?

A: We advise to hold on to a Christian faith and do not allow the groups to take power. Ireland is losing the Christianity in Europe. It is now a power in governments in investments and all in favour of the country on a commercial note. This is ok but we warn: it is playing with danger for power in these groups, as they will if they can brain wash, get money and try to rise above the Christian faith. This is the warning today Nollaig, highlight it soon if you can in Ireland please. People must not be said by the governments as they are trying to get in with these group and countries. Ireland has always been strong in democracy and in faith. Losing now within Europe. As Europe has changed Ireland's view on religion. Ireland is now growing too fast and costly and the influx of these Muslim and mixed religious groups could tilt the balance.

N: Much gratitude, I will pass this information on.

Do Something Before it's Too Late

Fear is the absence of love

A: Today we come with unconditional love to all mankind. Love allows one to get out of the ego and out of the way. Love allows the power that made the body to heal the body. This is when transformation takes place. When light and information flow. This is love.

Fear is only the absence of love. When healing the self or others. Do not have attachments. Do not have fear. Just healing from the universe, plain and simple. Always say prayers of gratitude, not just prayers of request. Above all trust Atlantis and 'St. Germain' working hard in this great transformation plan. This millennium is a change of consciousness. This is the important message for mankind for today and the future. Is the message clear?

N: Yes, as always in gratitude.

A: Our manuscript needs to be in the market place now, as this is the correct time for our communications to the world. We request these sacred writings, written over the years to be shared now. Then we will continue with very important information for the future. Do you understand?

N: Yes.

Evolution in Africa

A: Today we come to wish you well in this great work as always. It is not easy; we appreciate but very fruitful and rewarding in many ways. We would now like to warn of the coming events in Africa. The torture is getting worse now and in time things will change on a large scale. It must happen to the good of the people. It must be highlighted in the world now and when these dictators are brought to justice, it will be easier. It must happen in Africa as part of evolution and these countries must evolve now at this time in the raising of the earth's vibration. This cannot continue in the old ways of pure dictatorship as it resonates on a lower vibration. Newness is very important at this time on earth in openness in giving back power to the people in all countries and in all ways. Dictatorship will not win in this time. Do you understand?

N: Not really, please clarify.

A: Dictatorship is over now; it was the fear-based way of the world. At this time on earth it is prayer, light, raising the vibration and these dictators will be taken out for good, this is true like Saddam Hussein, and the regimes are over now. Do you understand my child?

N: Yes, but what can people do about this?

A: You can, through us send light and warn the people of our messages. Tell them to repent now, turn back to God and all will come in line. No falsehood now in any dealings, only truth will win. This will always be the case from now on. Keep counsel on Atlantis knowledge and keep calm. As it is in calmness that we can communicate with and through you. Write, print and go on the road with 'Atlantian workshops'. Farewell for now. your Atlantian friends in spirit.

N: Farewell and thank you.

Coming Events in Ireland 2008-2010

A: Things will slow down in a very profound way and people will begin to panic in debt, borrowing etc. The time is correct for souls to stop, recognise divinity in each soul and to find their correct mission in life. Commercialism is taking over and it must be balanced with the spiritual aspect of the person. It is important to know that in time people will look for a deeper meaning in life, not receiving now from the church. The church is doing great work but not connecting the soul to the correct path, simply because of dominance and dictatorship and commercialism in a way within the structure of its foundation.

It must change. We would like to point out that priests are ok, well educated and from fine backgrounds but unfortunately some are caught up in materialism wants and losing the humbleness in a sense. This is necessary in a childlike way to touch the people and to bring light to situations. Self healing is in the soul when in truth, being in self truth, we stress is the most important thing to remember. People are offloading to priests and this relieves them in a way but work must be done now in this particular time on earth on each individual soul in order to go forward in the new era of purification. This includes the healing of priests and bishops, and all souls.

N: How will purification come about please?

A: By means of cleansing as we have said before. It is necessary now to move the stuck souls into a more enlightened way of being. A great chance is available now to all who are listening. Light is needed on earth now; it is essential as darkness is strong in influence and things will and must happen to quieten mankind. This is our message for today. Go in peace, tune in later, important information coming in relation to the east in connection with control.

A: Thank you for this valuable wisdom of Atlantis.

China and Control

A: Nollaig, we greet you now with much light and gratitude for helping in this great work at this time on the planet. We understand fully the physical demands and the vibration lowering pull in many ways etc but we would like to advise the following:

In time you will understand much about our work, lifestyles, teachings, our ways, our downfall, our mistakes and you will know that we are warning for the good of mankind. Now mankind does not realise the urgency in this great work.

China will in time control eastern countries and this is not good for the world.

N: What will happen please?

A: Power and control is their agenda, only power in the world is their aim and this is what they want to achieve. The world looks up to this country but be warned, they will try to control the oil and they will try to influence the eastern countries and they wish to control all.

N: Should the world trade with them, yes or no?

A: No, not at the moment, highlight their ways and regime and control as seen in Burma that is horrific in the world. The killing of innocent souls no freedom and no values in self. This is a country that needs outside help.

N: How please?

A: Well by means of highlighting now during these times, Tibet is the same, all under control by regimes.

N: How can the world help in this?

A: By highlighting people, they should stop the business with these countries, Bangkok and the Olympics show china for what it does to its subjects and warn United Nations. The UN should do more to help out in Burma. Once again climate is highlighting these places, poverty stricken and taking those souls out both good and evil, through earthquakes etc. In time people will begin to understand and go forward in a new fresh approach in a more loving Godly way, but this evil in the world is coming to a head now. You can highlight the things to come as follows: war in North Korea, still a threat with USA, this is on the cards as we have mentioned before and it will cause much outrage in west. Governments are not helping in this, Korea/USA all in competition, and east v west. In time Korea will link with other eastern countries.

N: Is it China, yes or no?

A: China, and the power with all combined will be too strong for the west to handle and this will lead to an imbalance in the world. The people will not like this.

N: Should I warn in a book?

A: Yes, you will tell people of this and it must be made known, is that clear?

N: Yes it is crystal clear, in gratitude as always.

A Time to Come in Line

A Change in Consciousness

A: Today we wish to discuss the raise in consciousness on a global level. In days of old, nations were cultured in many ways and more spiritually advanced than today's civilization. It is time to listen to the wise old souls of Atlantis. We had a real spiritual insight with a devotion to sense. Our sacred teachings relate to the mysteries of heaven. Mankind must be loyal to the truth now and in doing so each individual will carve the way to rising up of consciousness on earth on a collective level.

We would like at this time to congratulate you on your work. Now you must be firm in printing material. We require that our sacred writings will be made available in:

- **Schools**
- **Churches**
- **Libraries**
- **All educational areas for humanity**

This is very important in delivering the message of Atlantis to the:

- **Youth**
- **General Public**
- **Church leaders (if allowed)**

They need to open up a little and trust in our information from the Godly source and adhere to the same. Do you understand?

N: Not really, please clarify on the church?

Church needs to humble itself at the core

A: Well the core of the organisation needs to humble itself and allow a newness, freshness in deliverance of the Holy Spirit to the congregation, to all age groups but in particular to the youth. They need counselling and firm handling. In time the organisation will understand this and will have to step back and allow, listen to and be as Jesus was on earth, amongst the people. Laying on of hands, out and about more in their work, if the people do not go to them they must change direction and work in a more relaxed, mobile, charismatic way in connection with their own truth and bring out the same in their flock. What is required in this area will take working at, but it will be rewarding all round.

More women are needed in this area. Female to balance the energy here. More women to connect with families to visit and to counsel in schools, in churches, in parishes. To reach out to the children and help to connect to the church through love, not fear as in old times. All fear should be abolished now at the dawning of a new age.

The Church is going through a transformation, this is necessary after the errors made. The people will know this and feel the pain in the vibration of all wrong-doings. The vibration is going to raise up now but truth has to be the ultimate in the broader spectrum of religion. This we want to emphasise. People are far to evolved now and this must be acknowledged in the church, so work must be done now in co-operation with the:

- **People**
- **Priests**
- **Bishops**

The Pope must liaise with governments, scientific research in the understanding of:

- **Individuality**
- **The planet and global warming**
- **Animals**
- **Teaching by example**

By humbling the Church we mean:

Property

A waste in property while some individuals are homeless. Sell to raise funds, put funds into research and mobile units to reach and not preach we stress, and involve the people in projects that will allow the Holy Spirit to reign once again – in love, in light and in peace on earth. This is the way forward in religion, respecting the soul's choice, in all ways through free will and allowing it to grow in truth when truth, and only when truth is recognised by all in the Church.

This is a wonderful time for growth

2009 – 2012 and beyond through saintly help

A: Collective awakening in truth will bring about a new Golden Age lost over time through negativity caused by mankind. Do you understand?

N: Yes, anything else on this topic please?

A: We would like to discuss the future comings of Saints.

Saints are helping now with those in truth and the time is correct to ask (only when in Self- Truth) for the salvation of past errors in all. It will be allowed when acknowledged. Is this information clear?

N: No, please clarify.

A: Saints have the power and ability to help mankind. They have lived in earthly bodies and they understand very well the short comings of all, this is so my child.

We wish to stress that they want to help, so allow this at this time on earth. Do you understand our teachings on saints?

N: Yes, in gratitude.

President of USA Barrack Hussain Obama

A: America's new President will be a great leader in communication with all. In self soul's journey in understanding the youth in an openness that is needed in the USA, but he needs to get firm with dictators that are still out there at large, waiting to bring him down, in old thinking in the United States of America. He is going to bring many changes quickly to the USA. Some will not be accepted by the people and some will. He needs to be very careful in his work as he is a target of the Eastern Countries.

In time he will be known for his uniqueness in work, in women in congress and in electing a more worthy government in change. He will win in USA for a time and a quick turn in his views, his way is unique but it will affect some and he may not get the chances as black people may try to dominate and this could lead to a conflict within USA as some white people will find it difficult to take. This is so, a type of racial war in a sense.

He is a good man in purity in a difficult position on a world stage. His values, his ways and his commitment are all excellent but USA needs light and he is a part of rising up to this in his understanding of his values in his mission. The people could cause problems and he will find it difficult in times ahead to keep to his policy. It is indeed all part of America's transformation. He will be wonderful in communications in the Middle East relations but in danger to regimes. A target on a peace mission, time will tell. His work and his path is a difficult one, he needs to be hands on at all times to hold the values that his campaign has won. USA needs to Stop War to take back western power now to be an example to the world while protecting the west at the same time from Korea. Diplomacy will be necessary with his government, that is all.

N: How long will he be leader for please?

A: Not long term as we have stated, he is part of the transition in raising the vibration. Three to four years perhaps.

N: I give thanks for information received.

My understanding of nine (9) in numerology is movement, unconditional love, unselfishness and working for the common welfare, patience, universality, tolerance and successful settlement/contracts etc. Is this what we are aspiring to in 2009?

A: Yes, this will take time to achieve in all souls but is possible now.

N: I will pass on your words of wisdom in much gratitude for information received.

Through Commitment Our Essence will Win

Please Commit to our Mission 2010

Our message today is one of commitment.

Affirmation for mankind to evolve and raise the vibration

"Affirmation"

I commit myself to the will of God

I give my heart and soul to God

I deserve the best in life

I serve the best cause in life

I am a divine manifestation

A: This is our request from mankind; if it resonates with a soul then the soul is awakening and ready to help in this great rewarding work at this time on earth. As we approach a new decade it is urgent and it is essential in the raising up of the vibration. Do you understand the request?

N: Yes, but I need clarification on the souls please – if the soul does not resonate with the affirmation does it have a lesson to learn?

A: Yes, a good question as always, free will and free choice. Do not push anybody, as the self truth combined with commitment is the key. Is that clear my child?

N: Yes, that clarifies things for me in gratitude as always.

A: Very well then, we will continue. We want this final year in our writings to hold a tone of hope for this time for all living on planet earth.

We wish to advise on the urgency once again on giving back to the planet.

Nourish the earth that gives life force.

Salute the divinity within all beings and above all be grateful for today as tomorrow is not yet yours. Each soul is on a journey, sometimes the correct path, sometimes not. We, the Atlantean lost civilisation, want to help now. A new age is dawning; please help in this great time of transformation. Many graces will be showered upon you who commit to our mission in the circles of light, transformation and truth. We have a vision for America to rise above and guide the world once again in the coming years. Raising the vibration is all important now in all mankind. Please accept our help from the spirit world as discussed in 2009. The free will and free choice always stand here. We advise for a golden age, return to work together all nations, all religions all governments as this is the only way forward.

Nuclear Gases

A: All nuclear power must now be blocked by the United Nations, we advise strongly on this issue in a very vulnerable planet and in the purity of its inhabitants. All are at risk from the threat of countries dealing in this type of energy; there is a better way to evolve.

(With reference to year 2005 titled 'Matrix of the Planet' - page 97)

The year 2011 will bring very strong winds, high oceans, disease in the Southern Hemisphere, conflict with races, water shortage in Africa and much more information to follow later. When information to date is published, many blessings to all who read our sacred writings and in particular to those who participated in this great plan of transformation into the Golden Age returning again to planet earth. Each soul is unique, in its essence and blessings to those who are not ready yet to help in this wonderful time of evolvement. We also send our blessings and acknowledgement with references to the particular stage of the soul's journey. At this point we will finish our conversation in much gratitude for your co-operation in our sacred writings from, as always, the Christ Essence St Germain.

To be continued...

Testimonials

Testimonial

As a hands-on Spiritual Healer, I have known Nollaig McKeogh BSYA (CoI) since 1999. Nollaig is founder of the Holistic Support Therapy Exchange and works with a gracious and moving manner in Reiki circles and meditation.

Her healing experience as an Aura-Soma Colour Therapeutic, Nollaig's consultation allows us to look at deep spiritual, emotional and physical issues in our lives.

The mirror of the soul:
I have worked with Nollaig at Knock, County Mayo, where many healing experiences have taken place. I have worked at Nollaig's workshops in Sligo. Her healing abilities have now taken her further afield to Spain.

With God's help may you continue with your generous profession of healing and helping others for many years ahead. It is a pleasure for all to work with you.

Philip Coogan D.Sc, MNFSH.
Author; Out Of The Flames.
www.outoftheflames.org

Open Testimonial

7th July 2008

Dear Nollaig

Many thanks for sending this poem for me to read. You are obviously a very thoughtful, expressive person and have been moved by the situation in Burma and AungSanSuki. I have really enjoyed reading this; it is very touching when a student goes that little bit further when studying this course.

Thank you for sharing your thoughts through this poem. I hope you don't mind but I have kept a copy.

I wish you all the best for the future and thank you for your contribution to the course. I have really enjoyed working with you

With Best Wishes
Adele
The Open University

Testimonial

My Reiki Incitation with Nollaig released negativity. "I love dancing" I now have more self confidence in my ability to: (A) teach dancing and (B) combine the art of healing with the creative art of dancing. The world needs healing on a collective level, this I know and this is true, I also know of my ability to heal and counsel on many levels. There is a time on earth for each soul to evolve and through the free will and choice on a soul level, I will know when the time is correct for me.

Muchas Gracias
Kath of KT'S Line Dancers
La Manga, Spain

Testimonial

Hola,

During a healing session on Christmas Day 2004, Nollaig received the spiritual message that that my blood was stagnant. After a visit to the doctor, a blood test and a short stay in hospital, Deep Vein Thrombosis was diagnosed. Whatever she says comes true.

Adiós
Vincentia
San Miguel, Spain

Testimonial

I first met Nollaig at a 'Mind, Body & Soul Day' in Orihuela Costa. I was drawn to her stand "Atlantis". As she explained about Atlantis to me so I purchased The Crystal Cross Meditation. I became very interested and decided to telephone her, which resulted in being taught Reiki One and Two and Seichem. Also I became involved with The Circles of Light which I have been doing for about two years every week on Wednesday at 9 o' clock. We send the light to Countries, religion and the planet.

Since being involved with the above I have found contentment.

Anita Bucknall
Spain

Testimonial

The Crystal Cross Mediation takes me to a quiet place, voice is calm and mecodre. Attention drawn to protection is very important regarding awareness in the general public. Well done! It must have taken ages to prepare.

Oh! The music at the end was wonderful.

Julia Marafe
Crystal Workshop Teacher & Healer
London

Testimonial

I found the channelling to be a great comfort to me during a time of stress, and it has proven to be correct so far in my life.

Belief in the source is important, coupled with the correct chosen person for this unique gift, and above all, trust.

Thank you.

Deirdre
Co-Tipperary, Ireland

Testimonial

A spiritual message received to the biggest little woman in the world. It came true 100 per cent, in more ways that I could ever imagine.

I received healing as I was angry with the nuns, having spent 15 years with my eldest sister in an orphanage – great punishment was inflicted upon us. Forty-seven years later, it came back to enlighten me on my sister's passing (1994). I knew I was on a mission as I felt alive inside and dead outside. I experienced a re-birth, something special happened, my anger at the nuns disappeared and I blossomed. What started in darkness became a bright star. What better way to remember somebody? My project started with music and finished with a star.

Thanks for your spiritual guidance.

Miriam Tralee
Co-Kerry, Ireland

Testimonial

Dermot has come to me in the form of a bird. A dove, symbol of peace, deliverance and forgiveness. His message was clear and to the point. "I've spoken to cousin Nollaig, please stop worrying about me, please set me free, I want to fly like a bird." These were the words of my only son Dermot who recently past to the spirit. May he rest in peace now. A pigeon in need of attention arrived on my balcony the next morning. I felt a strong connection to this bird, fed and watered it. The next day it took flight. The holy spirit works in many ways. I felt the presence and the healing in the whole experience. This therapeutic story is yours to do as you wish with it.

Thank you
Sheila Douds
Eastbourne, UK

Testimonial

I just have to let you know that we are coming over to Ireland to support you for the launch of your new book "Conversations with Atlantis".

Thank you for your friendship and guidance. It has been invaluable in my decisions and gave me strength in my times of need. I will add your book to my website.

Barbara Blaylock
Southampton UK
The Healthy Chocolate Revolution
www.slimmersdreamchocolate.com

Poetry & Meditation

The Atlantian Plight
December 2003 – 2013

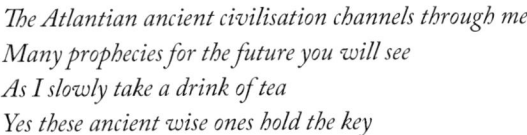

It is the month of December
A wonderful time to reflect and remember
This year is 2003
Jesus Christ was born to save both you and me.

The Atlantian ancient civilisation channels through me
Many prophecies for the future you will see
As I slowly take a drink of tea
Yes these ancient wise ones hold the key

Lost in the tidal waves in the past
It all happened so fast…
A destructive force exploded in the sea
Today it can happen to you or me
Perhaps it was the way it was meant to be

Volcanoes erupted on a very large score
As tidal waves engulfed our continent
And swallowed up our shores
Some escaped to Egypt, would you like to know more?
We were a very highly evolved race
Of today there is very little trace

Things will happen on the planet
To make people stop and take note
The following we are about to quote
Seas will riise…Mankind you will hear their cries
Global warming and tidal waves and much, much more
This is what is in store

Time will speed up, as the world is moving faster
There are so many issues to master
This world is in a state of disaster
This information is only a starter
As war, quakes, floods are in store
And much, much more

Things are going to collapse
The monetary system in Europe perhaps
Don't get caught up in this greedy world
Climate is going to distress many
This might all sound a bit canny

Seas are rising now as we communicate
Ice is melting at a high fast furious rate
Please ask humanity to do something before it's too late

Our western democracy is still in much danger
To the planet Atlantis is no stranger
The balance is titled in a much negative way
What more can we say….but call on the Almighty every day
Or the ultimate price like us….all mankind will pay

This is the Atlantian plight
You must all put up a great fight
It is time to let in the light

©Nollaig McKeogh

Flooding in New Orleans

The water rose in New Orleans
This crazy world is not always as it seems
With prisoners rioting
Black and white folk fighting
The whole area now needs light

Atlantians sunk this is so
The world today needs to flow in order to grow
New Orleans is at an all time low to Miami and Ohio, many will escape.
It is all to do with the new worlds shape
New Orleans is a lesson to many citizens about neglect
As the Government through its people choose Bush with regret

It is time to let go now, change is imminent
To the neighbouring states the people will flee
This is only the start of what you will see
Music will in time lift the vibration

To her people we wish to say move without hesitation
And in time to the almighty like us they will have more dedication
Please pass this on from the Atlantians who sunk in
floods and tidal waves through greed and progress

Nollaig
Atlantis

A: New Orleans is like we were in the beginning of the floods, many were lost, and some fled as we have said to Egypt. Animals were lost; the Continent of Atlantis is still under water, to be found in the future by archaeologists.

N: Where is it please?

A: South of the Azores is the location in the Atlantic, some fled to Africa, Egypt and Spain. Some died, refugees… we were refugees like some today. We sank through greed of progress. This is happening in America. Greed is the ruination of all and trying to be better than other countries. The world is bad in competition.

Countries and religions should pull together and help one another. America is taking form the East and is the power behind the west. England is going to gain in Europe. England will learn many lessons as a type of Karma created by dominance in the past, that is all my child.

Ref: Poem on New Orleans
Shalom
Jacob

Innismurray Island

He smiled and a fisherman's wisdom shone through
This island is sacred what we can do
Like an emerald jewel in the wild Atlantic
This is so true; the purity in its isolation is a bonus too

Innismurray essence is linked to the great pyramids in Egypt we know
Via Carnac in France, it's possible to row
This island needs a chance
The Heritage Committee may build an interpretative ranch
The island is needed to enhance our land
The Irish people should now lend a hand
To restore this jewel in the wild Atlantic
As Europe influences Ireland
We are losing our lush green land

A pilgrim holistic site for all to enjoy
Recharge our batteries and tune into Éireann soul past
Allowing dolphins to come and explore
Would help therapeutically to the earth's very core
This wonderful haven eliminates sacredness galore
We must respect the souls buried on shore
Along with its poteen legends, sweet honey and more

Nollaig
Atlantis

The Holistic Pathfinder
Be prepared for those whom you will meet
Please be discerning, as you are also learning
As our channel we would like to know

With your free will and our guidance you will grow
Sometimes it is important to go slow
There are many seeds to sow
As the souls aspire to the light

Some will put up a fight
At the free will and the lesson in sight
But keep on this holistic path
And in time ahead
The Golden Age will spread
Greed, Power and Ego will ultimately be dead

Received December 18th 2004

(A Special Birthday treat for our earthly channel)

Nollaig
Atlantis

Angel of Burma

The Burmese people are dying
Yet, from China the world continues buying
The military junta continue their lying
Nobel peace prize winner Aung San Suu Kyi
Leader for the democratic Burmese government
In the future it is possible to see
A voice for her now...is the ultimate key
Humanity is suffering it could eventually effect you or me
The world needs urgently to stop and see
The dangers from east and the powers that be

Nollaig
Atlantis

Burma

A: Burma is in a state of control and fear, this is not acceptable in the world. It is bad and people should speak out. These people understand now that this will not work on the current vibration.
Losing power in the eyes of the world.

N: Who please?

A: They will eventually give in and face the world.

A: The bullies in Burma, dictators and corrupt regimes. Losing all and not winning in this country.

N: Why do they not accept help from the western countries?

A: This is because it is in a pact with eastern countries and it is not Accepted in their worldly views and it will change with climate soon. Burma is not going to win with this government when released of powers. It will start to trigger outrage and split the country in the near future.
This will lead to an intervention with sanctions; then China will retaliate to this boycott and trouble will grow.

N: When please?

A: Next year perhaps 2009

N: I give thanks for this… Is there anything else?

A: You will know when to share information…

That is all on Burma.

Ref: Poem Angel of Burma

John Paul II

John Paul II left us quietly when God beckoned

Genuinely missed by all
You quietly answered your call

Gone to a vibration above our imagination
A wonderful gift lost to all nations
As you mingle with all and Diana (Princess of Hearts)
This is where your new journey starts
Freedom at last from the bondage of physical pain
In your latter years you began to show the strain
From your guidance we mankind had so much to gain

Touched by your simplicity, in a cypress coffin you were lain
Not one thing about you was at all vain
In our new shepherd Benedict we must confide
You now have more power from above to guide
When all is said and done
We your flock must carry on
We know in our hearts, you have not really gone
Now a saint, many hearts you have won

Nollaig
Atlantis

The Berlin Wall

The Berlin Wall tumbled in 1989
This is all part of evolution
Our governments must find the solution
As asylum seekers queue up at Dover
For poor old England it is now all over

From madmen they are fleeing
We must not discourage on our meeting
Some are good, some bad, some OK
Who are we to say?
We must allow them the time of day

To western Europe refugees will elope
This is not a joke
As most of them hang on to hope
Some even respect the Pope

They choose asylum in Spain
As they do not like the rain
Some choose France if given the chance
Others travel to Ireland it's free and easy
Bertie provides the tea and more
As they receive our hospitality... galore

They know their entitlements, that is true
Some are even out to sue
They will pick our economy's brains if they can
But from their own countries they ran
Their culture needs to be integrated with ours
The new growing Europe certainly have the powers

Nollaig
Atlantis

Superbug MRSA

As a loved on in agony passes away
We know in our hearts it was the MRSA
Our health board is crumbling round us in decay
It is not before time, to keep this superbug at bay

It crosses my mind almost every day
The ultimate price a humble soul had to pay
I suppose in a way, it could happen to anyone
In a hospital for a very short stay

The time is correct now to highlight the truth…
Of this superbug MRSA we must get to the root
As on the death cert there is a lie
In time to come the western health board will eat humble pie
This poem must be adhered to before many more folk die

Nollaig
Atlantis

A tribute to Margaret, my mother-in-law, a highly evolved soul who suffered greatly. On her death certificate it simply said 'pneumonia'. It had been confirmed by a nurse that she had died from MRSA, showing all symptoms of this deadly infection. She handled her pain with great dignity and prayer, her immune system broke down and she eventually caught pneumonia. May she rest in peace and enjoy the light.

A: MRSA superbug needs to be highlighted within the hospitals in Ireland and the UK. It is killing many people as they are vulnerable to this infection. Hospitals need to admit the truth.

N: Do you mean sue the hospitals as some do?

A: No that is not the way. It is not on our vibration, the health board needs money and also needs to be truthful.

Atlantis

A Crystal Cross Meditation

Awaken your crystalline body

The crystal cross meditation is a meditation channelled through, for this time of our evolution here on earth.

From the ancient and wise civilisation the Atlantians who mined crystals and knew of their therapeutic healing powers.

The last Atlantian civilisation in the end sunk themselves through misuse of technology. They wish to warn mankind now. Please listen to their words of wisdom and prophecies direct from God. Mankind is in danger of repeating history on earth today,

Best results are achieved here by collecting your chakra set of crystal and incorporating them into your family life.

*Crystals can be used for protection around your computer
*Worn as a piece of jewellery
*Placed in the home to raise the vibration

Meditation

- Relax yourself into a comfortable position, taking a long deep breath. Feel the energy in the base chakra associated with mineral kingdom and element earth.

- As you breathe into this centre, visualise the colour red. Pick up a red jasper crystal, holding it in your left hand. Connect with this crystal; allow it to help with your ideas and thoughts. Notice how you feel.

- Now lay it aside and taking a good deep breath, visualise the colour orange around your naval associated with the plant realm and element water. Now bend down and pick up a crystal carnelian, holding it in your left hand. Become attached to it. Feel it bringing in the orange vibration, cleansing your emotions. Lay it aside, beside the red crystal.

- On your next breath, breathe in the colour yellow and feel your solar plexus fill with yellow, opening out into a sunflower.

- As you bend down to pick up a citrine crystal, feel at one with this energy and visualise the colour flowing out through the tips of your fingers. Now place it aside.

- On your next deep breath, pick up a rose quartz crystal with the message of unconditional love to your heart centre. Now place the rose quartz crystal aside.

- On your next deep breath, breathe in the colour blue. Visualise the colour all around your throat centre. We are now in a time of collective communication. Release the colour blue and lay it down beside the other crystals.

- Taking a deep breath, breathe in the colour indigo right into the centre of the forehead. As you pick up a crystal to resonate with this chakra, tune into its frequency. Does it have a message? Notice how you are feeling.

- Now on the next breath, breathe in the colour violet, just above the crown chakra and as you do, pick up an ametheyst crystal allowing it to bring in the healing colour of violet, bringing about transformation on all levels. Place the crystal down beside the others and notice how the seven crystals form a crystal rainbow and all the colours of the spectrum as they bring about balance to your whole being.

- On your next breath rise above the crown chakra and visualise pure white light flowing down and just be. Be in the brilliance of the white light. Now pick up a clear quartz crystal.

- On a deep breath, breathe in white light up and up, through all your chakra centres and out through the top of the head. As you do, the white light takes the form of a cross. The cross takes the form of four triangles; one facing downwards, one facing upwards, and on each side meeting in the centre, joined by a circle. Look into the cross, right into the circle into the centre. Does it have a message for you, a colour or perhaps a symbol? Breathe into the energy of this sacred space and be. Just be in the light of the cross, drawing strength and support from it.

- As the cross fades away, you descend back along the chakra path. Balancing your upper and lower bodies. Fill your heart with unconditional love. (It is in this space the Atlantian essence can communicate when in truth)

- Now move down through the yellow orange, down deeper and visualise the deep red colour grounding with a magnetic pull to the earth.

- You are now back in the physical, and the brilliant white light is all around your body, creating many circles of white light. Hold onto this image. Acknowledge the crystal cross. Become the crystal cross, allowing the light to heal and protect your aura.

The 8th Meditation

Spirit: Meditate balance with divinity

Physical: Linking your spirit and your physical and centring in your heart through music, light, truth and colour

8 recommendations for meditation

1. **Create your sacred space.**
2. **Change thinking to positive thoughts.**
3. **Raise consciousness.**
4. **Select a comfortable chair or sit on the floor with a straight back.**
5. **Choose soothing music.**
6. **Condition your mind to meditation.**
7. **Commitment is the key, make that commitment.**
8. **Circle. If in a group, all members must be in pure thought form. Negative energy will drain away from the group.**

Meditation

Sit quietly, gather your thoughts. Now ask yourself are my thoughts of use to me or are they holding me back? Then, taking a good deep breath, hold to the count of eight. Release your breath deep down into the solar plexus. Notice how you are feeling. Now breathe into the energy. What are your issues? Taking a long deep breath once again and hold to the count of eight, allowing your worries and issues into the light to a higher vibration for cleansing. Release once again deep down into the solar plexus (your nervous energy centre just above your navel). Breathe into this energy centre. Are there any mothering issues, marital, childhood issues, etc? Any worries and anxieties, whatever they may be, taking a long deep breath and hold to the count of eight. Notice the figure eight lit up and shining. You are looking out of the top section of the figure eight. Release once again and continue this process for 10 to 15 minutes per day. Make that enlightening connection with the figure eight and rise above conflict in your physical body.

From CD Bridging the Gap between Holistic and Conventional Medicine in Europe
Compiled by Dr A Cisneros, Spain and Nollaig McKeogh, Ireland

The Planet in the eyes of an eight year old

By Lauren Gough

Our Planet

I look around me
What do I see?
Our planet needs help
It's as clear as can be
I support the planet
And the planet supports me
Working together is the key
They Holy Spirit shines a bright ray
Keeping all evil away
Each person must absorb the light
And help our planet in its worthy plight

Glossary

Atlantis
A lost city said to have existed before the Greeks and Egyptians after the Lemurians. It was a continent inhabited by highly intelligent people who knew about atomic energy, the principles of light and the power of crystals.

Channelling
Channels are usually conscious when information is being received. The vibration must be high in the channel's energy field in order to connect with the highly evolved masters; St Germain in this book. It is important to be in the self true and positive. Channelled material often contains important messages for mankind, as in *Conversations with Atlantis*.

Dolphins
Some people believe that dolphins are the most highly evolved creatures on earth, with great healing powers. They are here to teach us and to help us to evolve, care for each other and the planet. There is a strong rapport between humans and these wonderful creatures. Swim with the dolphins, it is a wonderful healing and spiritual experience - you won't regret it.

Jacob
Son of Isaac, grandson of Abraham. Dreamt about a stairway to heaven with angels going up and down and the Lord standing beside it. From book of Genesis GBN.

Scribe
A person who wrote documents in days of old. Scribes were employed by ancient kings to prepare official documents.

Prophecies
This is the ability to predict events before they happen. Prophets usually receive messages form the Holy Spirit. Most prophecies relate to world events, wars and disasters etc, or the good news of a birth. Famous ancient prophets include Moses, Isaiah and those who proclaim the word of God. The New Testament speaks of prophets in the early church. John the Baptist is also called a prophet.

Notes

Notes

Questionnaire

1. Who is your favourite writer? _____
2. Do you enjoy poetry reading? Yes ☐ No ☐
3. Would you like to attend poetry reading? Yes ☐ No ☐
4. Are you a member of a writers group? Yes ☐ No ☐
5. How often are writers circles held in your local area?

   Please tick appropriate box

   Weekly ☐ Monthly ☐ Quarterly ☐ Annually ☐ Don't Know ☐

6. Are you a member of:

   A book club ☐

   A local library ☐

7. How many books have you read in the last year? _____
8. Are you Aware of Atlantis Lost Civilization? Yes ☐ No ☐
9. If answer is 'yes' do you have a question
   (in relation to you soul's journey)?

   _____

10. Are you interested in planetary healing? Yes ☐ No ☐
11. Please insert your telephone no. _____

©Nollaig McKeogh (087) 6961618

Conversations with Atlantis

Email: Channel4Atlantis@googlemail.com

Post questionnaire to: Moon Publishing, Carrowkeel view, Laragan, Collooney, Co-Sligo, Ireland